Circles of Light

MEMORIES OF AN ISLAY CHILDHOOD

James Knox Whittet

The Islands Book Trust

LIVING HISTORY

THE ISLANDS BOOK TRUST
URRAS LEABHRAICHEAN NAN EILEAN

Published in 2024 by the Islands Book Trust

Islands Book Trust, Community Hub, Balallan, Isle of Lewis,
HS2 9PN. Tel: 07930 801899

https://islandsbooktrust.org/

Typeset by Erica Schwarz (www.schwarz-editorial.co.uk)
Printed and bound by Martins the Printers, Berwick upon Tweed, UK

ISBN: 978-1-907443-88-6

Front cover image depicts the Paps of Jura at sunset.

Photos by kind permission of Ann Knox Whittet, Margaret Bathgate,
Greig Morrison, Donald James MacPhee and 'Old Islay' Facebook page.

Dedicated to my sisters and brother: Isabel, Catherine, Muriel,
George – and to my wife, Ann

We look at the world once, in childhood.
The rest is memory.

Louise Glück

James Knox Whittet was born and brought up on the Hebridean island of Islay where his father was the head gardener at Dunlossit Castle.

After leaving the island, he was educated at Newbattle Abbey College and Cambridge University. James has a passion for islands and he edited the first ever island anthology, *100 Island Poems of Great Britain and Ireland* (Iron Press), which won a major award from the Arts Council who funded a reading tour to a range of islands from Jersey to Islay. This was followed by the prose anthology, *Writers on Islands* (Iron Press).

His poetry collections include *Poems from The Hebrides*, *Voices and Images of Islay*, *When Kafka Met Einstein* and *A Life Beyond Walls: Poems and Images from the Holy Land*.

James has won awards for his poetry and was twice winner of the Neil Gunn Memorial Award for writing.

Although James now lives with his wife, Ann, in a small village in Norfolk, his siblings remain in Scotland with a sister and extended family still living on Islay.

Contents

Contents

FOREWORD

The book is wistful, poetic and evocative of a time and a place. I personally know Dunlossit and Port Askaig and Keills, the principal locations of this memoir, but it also brought back my own recollections of life as a 5/6 year old in Port Ellen on the other side of the island of Islay.

But this account does more than just trigger memories of my long-lost youth. It is a treasure chest of sentiments close to most of us who are of a certain age. Many will read it, reminded of that point in life when Primary School was comfortable, when the move to Secondary School was a momentous leap of faith and where the summers were full of undisturbed, but not always innocent, activity.

I was especially caught by the description of the nightmare 'holiday' with the stormy journey on the ferry from Tarbert to Gourock. I can still vividly recall many journeys on the Islay ferry, the *Lochiel*, and I was to see it finally moored at rest far away in Bristol harbour.

This is a lyrical and magnetic account of a boyhood on a wonderful Hebridean island. It is absorbing and moving. I could not stop reading.

Rt Hon Lord Robertson of Port Ellen KT GCMG
*Former UK Secretary of State for Defence
and 10th Secretary General of NATO*

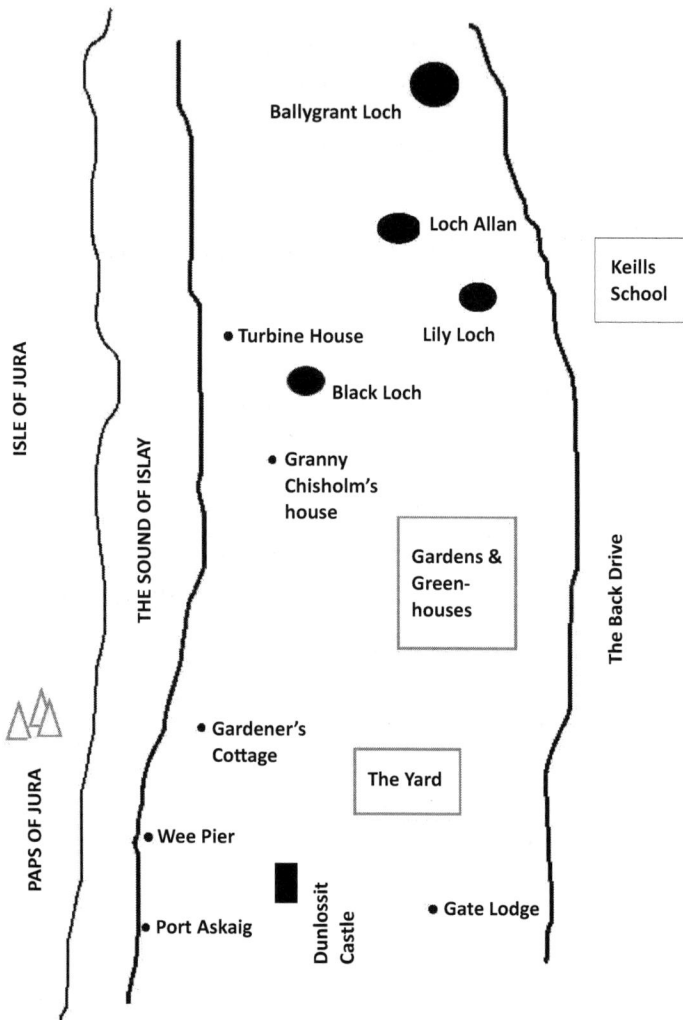

The author's remembered map of Dunlossit in diagram form

CHAPTER I

Entering into Light

My very first memory is of entering into dazzling light. It's so difficult to remember the precise age at which any event occurred in infancy but I think that I may have been aged around two. I seem to recall that I had been carried downstairs and taken into the kitchen and it was there that I experienced an overwhelming sense of light. It is a memory which has stayed with me throughout my life and which has coloured it as this appeared to be my first conscious moment of seeing.

I have come to feel that what matters most in life is holding on to one's best moments, keeping faith with them, amid all the doubt, disappointment and anguish which life brings, and that very early experience was one of my best moments.

Our house was perched on a wooded cliff, looking down on the Sound of Islay with its rapid, ever altering currents. The light was constantly changing as it was reflected off the surface of the sea. Some mornings sun strands would dance off the sea. More often the Sound would look grey and restless and the strong winds would make the sea shiver as dark clouds raced above. On calmer days, with no sunlight, the sea would flow sluggishly and look sullen.

I felt that the moods of the sea affected my moods. When the surface of the sea was grey and restless, I also felt restless. When the sea was caressed by fingers of light, I felt hopeful and comforted.

The light was influenced by the brooding Paps of Jura across the Sound. I read later that those rounded peaks were regarded by the earliest islanders as the breasts of some maternal deity who looked benignly down on people and, as a child, I had the sense that they were watching over me. When I read years later that George Orwell had written much of *1984* while living on Jura, I was struck by the contrast between the maternal deity and the malign *Big Brother*, equally watchful but threatening.

From our house, the colour of the Paps was constantly changing, the smoothed peaks often shrouded by mist and drowning in drizzle. On other days, their flanks would be caressed by fugitive fingers of sunlight. In winter, their heads would be concealed by bridal veils of snow. I stared at those Paps and they stared right back at me.

On days of the highest tides, I would feel a shiver of fear, and a strange delight when the sea threatened to overflow the island. I remember being taken down the drive to stand above the pier at Port Askaig and watch the sea rise higher and higher until the surface of the pier was submerged. It was as if my whole world was drowning.

On moonlit evenings of autumn, the Sound would take on the glow of smelting silver through the trees. I traced the path of the moon on the sea with its layer after layer of light without end. On some autumn nights, the moonlit silence would be punctuated by the urgent barking of lusting stags which echoed across the Sound from the bare slopes of Jura, that island of deer. There was a ghostliness about those echoes like the distant calls of the lost. Some mornings, the drowned bodies of stags who had swum across the Sound in the urgency of their desire would be found on the rocks below our house. Their lifeless bodies washed by the waves as if they were laid out for burial.

In spring, the heather clad hills of Jura were set on fire and the fire lit up the night and was mirrored on the sea. It was as if the sea itself had caught fire. Those fires glowed like blazing sunsets. They seemed to appear suddenly without warning as if the heather had caught fire out of its own volition. As an infant I did not know that the fires were started deliberately by gamekeepers in order to create fresh heather shoots for red deer and grouse. I would hear the shouts of men echoing through the air as those fires grew out of their control and threatened to burn the entire island.

My infancy was a tapestry of ever-changing light.

CHAPTER 2

Stepping on to an Island

I was the youngest of a family of five, a belated mistake. In later times, the foetus that was me might well have been aborted. My conception was regarded as an act of shame as my mother was nearly forty years of age and this led my parents to move away from their friends and acquaintances in the area around Kilmelford in Argyllshire, to move to this island the existence of which they had been unaware of. I wonder what fears my mother must have experienced when she boarded a ferry for the first time in her life in Tarbert, Loch Fyne in the grey, November chill with, no doubt, the rain falling, forming reflecting puddles on the cracked concrete of the pier. She was never able to overcome her fear of the sea – to her it was always a source of dread. By boarding this boat to an unknown island, she was leaving behind all that she had ever known and it removed her still further from her family in the Borders where she had grown up at such a safe distance from the sea.

In the 1950s, the ferry called *The Lochiel* called in at Gigha and Jura on its way to Islay which lengthened the sail considerably and increased the likelihood of sea sickness for passengers prone to this distressing condition. As the ferry made its way through the Sound of Islay with its wake fading behind it, my family would have seen the bare slopes of Jura on one side and the gentle, green hills of Islay on the other side. As the *Lochiel* approached Port Askaig, if they had looked up, they would have caught a glimpse of the semi-detached, whitewashed cottage in which they were to live. Just a hundred yards or so further down, they would have seen the imposing Dunlossit Castle, as it was then called, with its reddish stone revealed between the trees, with *Virginia creeper* clambering up one side of the building which

3

deepened the red each autumn. On the flagpole, the Union Jack lengthening and shortening with each gust of sea wind.

After some three hours or more, my father, mother and their four children ranging in ages from two to ten: Isabel, the eldest, followed by Catherine, Muriel and George, would have made their way down the rickety gangway, burdened by suitcases, to set foot on the pier at Port Askaig – the port of ash trees – and begin their new life with more trepidation than hope. They would have stood and watched as lorries, cars and cargo were precariously winched off the ferry in a net, like trapped game, swinging out over the edge of the pier until they finally landed on safe ground, more or less intact. Finally, the van which contained their few pieces of furniture would be unloaded and driven a few hundred yards up the steep brae and over the cattle grid which rattled at every crossing, and along the limestoned drive, lined on both side with trees letting fall their leaves in readiness for winter. It would move past the castle and up the short, stony brae with its ditches choked with dead leaves, to the house in which they were to live for the next fourteen years and which was to be my home for the first thirteen and a half years of my life.

Dusk would have been descending on that autumn afternoon as they entered the house, and across the Sound the only light they would have seen from their kitchen window would have come from the house by the ferry jetty on Jura which is the emptiest of the larger Hebridean islands. They must have been struck by the immense darkness and wondered where on earth they had landed, so far from all that they had known.

Power cuts were frequent on Islay in the 1950s and 60s. The electricity wires and poles were unable to withstand the fierce winds that swept across the Atlantic Ocean to batter the island. Dunlossit Estate alone had thousands of acres of deciduous trees and each storm would bring down trees which would in turn bring down the electricity cables and many houses on the estate would be left in a darkness relieved only by the flickering fire from the hearth; candles balanced on saucers or the unsteady flame behind glass from the paraffin lamp which would cast lengthening shadows across the distempered ceiling of the kitchen. My father was never satisfied with the flame from the lamp which had a tendency to cast ragged rings of smoke. He would constantly lift the funnel from the lamp and trim the paraffin-soaked wick but still the rings of smoke would rise and the room would be filled with that odour of paraffin which now, almost more than anything else, evokes my childhood and that house above the sea watched over by the Paps across the Sound. Perhaps on that first night on the island the lights would have gone out and they would have groped their way up the uncarpeted stairs to bed, their footsteps echoing within unfamiliar walls.

CHAPTER 3

Taking my Chances

This was the world of sea, smoke and light into which I was born some six months later. My mother would not have attended any pre-natal appointments or classes, even if such things were available on the island, and unlike almost all expectant mothers on Islay today, she was not flown to a hospital in Glasgow in order to have her baby in a maternity ward with all the latest medical advances at her disposal. She may well not even have consulted the doctor whose surgery was some ten miles away in Bowmore. My birth was left for nature to take its course, until the last night when the doctor would have been reluctantly summoned, not knowing if the outcome would be life or death. I would have been dragged screaming into the world to take my chances in a small, chilly bedroom in that house where the sounds of the sea formed an ever changing, musical background to our lives. People of Gaelic heritage had long believed that where a person is born is where their soul resides and, if that is true, those not actually born on the island will not feel the same depth of love and spiritual attachment to the place.

Like many people, I suspect, I would like to delve into the first months and years of my life and bring out my earliest impressions, thoughts and feelings, but memory cannot reach so far back just as it cannot reach into those months before birth. And yet those earliest impressions may well influence the rest of one's life. When does consciousness begin? If it begins at the moment when one is born then it is our memory which is at fault and that is why we cannot relive those first two years or so of our lives.

Even after the age of two or three until the age of five or more, only fragments of my early childhood remain. One of my most vivid memories is seemingly being left entirely on my own one afternoon in summer when I think the rest of the family had gone to the high walled garden, some two hundred yards from our house, in which my father worked. Perhaps they had gone to pick gooseberries, blackcurrants or raspberries for the *Big House*, the name we gave to Dunlossit Castle. I was sitting at the card table with its folding legs and green baize top which I liked to run my fingers across as if I was stroking the fur of a cat. I had been given the present of small plastic farm animals which I was able to stand on the surface of the table and I would move them around into different groupings. I remember there were sheep, cows, donkeys and brown hens, rather like the hens belonging to the Chisholms who lived next door. I would see those hens sheltering beneath the drooping flowers of the fuchsia in our garden when it rained. Not only were there animals but white plastic fences and gates and I would lead the sheep and cows through those gates. I have rarely felt such moments of happiness and absorption as I sat at that card table in the kitchen flooded with the reflected light of the sea. I experienced a rare sense of peace and the feeling that I was in control of the world which I had myself created.

Another fragment of remembered infancy is of me playing 'houses' with my sisters and brother. We would create a clearing amid the rhododendron bushes which grew so profusely on Dunlossit Estate. In such a clearing, we would be sheltered from the pervasive wind which sounded day after day, making the branches of trees groan and the fingered leaves of the rhododendrons shiver, revealing their pale undersides. We would use empty tins of *Fray Bentos* Steak and Kidney pies, which my mother would carefully divide into seven portions. We would fill those tins with mud and leave them until they had dried and formed a crust. We would have a rusted kettle which had been thrown out when it began to leak. From this dripping kettle we would pour water onto the dark, peated earth and stir it with a stick as if making porridge. We were often more content in this imagined house than we were in the actual one.

Another favourite pastime was gathering fir cones at the end of summer and see which one of us could gather the most. Our wealth was measured in cones. I remember the texture of them in my small hands and remember the scent of them; as they dried, they would open and swell. I liked to watch my heap grow higher. I don't recall us doing anything with the cones. As a bibliophile delights in collecting books he will never read, I simply collected cones of differing shapes and sizes: the pleasure was in the collecting.

I would look forward to autumn as a child more than any other season. Autumn was the season of leaf bonfires which my father lit with rolled up copies of *The Oban Times* or *The Daily Express*. Part of his job as the gardener on the estate was to maintain the drive from our house down past the castle and on to the Gate Lodge at the end of the drive. In October, I would long for a dry day so that the fallen beech leaves could be burnt. I felt such an excitement seeing a match lit within my father's cupped hands; the sulphur smell and the wind-blown pages of the newspapers which blackened and curled as they were consumed by flames and the handful of not quite dry leaves gently dropped on the papers; the smoke rising in blue clouds into the misted autumn air.

My father moved further down the drive after each heap of leaves was lit, with the scrape of his wire rake on the limestone gravel. There would be fires burning all along the drive and as dusk descended early, each fire would glow with a deepening red and in the darkness the fires would shine like a row of stars. I would look down over Port Askaig pier and up the length of the Sound and see the lighthouse on Jura flash and flash through the darkness as if mirroring the lights of the leaf fires like answered prayers.

Another vivid memory of my early childhood was the walk I took with my sisters and brother on frosted nights with the moon ghosting the sea in the spaces between the trees and with the sky revealing its tapestry of stars. We experienced a childhood sense of wonder at just gazing up at the vastness of space – there was of course no light pollution. We would walk up the drive, past the two painted doors which led into the walled garden and around the house of the old lady we called 'Granny' Chisholm although she was not our granny but the mother of our next-door neighbour, and go back home along the narrower, grass crested lane. We would often follow that circular walk on nights transfigured by moonlight and starlight.

Granny once lived with her husband who was a retired gamekeeper who had worked for many years on Dunlossit Estate. He died not long after I was born and Granny was left to live alone in that large, gloomy house. My mother would visit her some afternoons and I would be taken, rather reluctantly, with her. We would walk along the lane, past the small, fuchsia fringed pond which dried up in summer to expose its surface of cracked mud. From behind the pond, hens would step gingerly out of the dilapidated hen house with lichen creeping along its rotting, wood panels. When the sun shone, flecks of rust could be seen falling from its tin roof. I liked to watch the hens stab their beaks into the dust for worms and grubs; I liked the fussy sounds they made to each other, like humans who are impatient with each other's inability to listen.

All too soon, we would reach the back door of Granny's house and my mother would knock, loosening green flecks of paint which fell on to the worn doorstep. Granny would slowly come to the door and welcome us into that gloomy, low-ceilinged living-room with a fire flickering in the grate even in summer. On the wall, was a sepia photograph of her late husband, resplendent in tweeds with a shotgun and a black Labrador at his side. Now, a greyish, Scottie dog drowsed by the fire with a dog bowl half-filled by the kitchen door. When the conversation between my mother and Granny died down, I would listen to the loud ticking of the grandfather clock measuring the time which always seem to slow in that house. After a decent interval, Granny would bring in tea and biscuits from the kitchen, the biscuits almost always soft and inedible and I would try to conceal the offered biscuit in my pocket, pretending that I had eaten it.

A few years later, I heard my parents whisper to each other that Granny was staying with her daughter next door to us and that she was being *eaten away*. From time to time, I would look up at the window of the bedroom she was in with a fearful wonder at what was taking place in that room. One morning, I looked up at that window and saw that the curtains were drawn and I later heard that she had died in the night. Time, however slowly it seemed to pass in that dark living-room with its smells of burning coal and ageing dog, had run out for her. I heard later that my father had to unhinge a door from the stable yard across the drive from our house to take Granny's body down the stairs which were too winding and narrow for a coffin. I would sometimes imagine her lifeless body stretched out on that door as it made its descent for the final time. The whisperings of my parents made death appear all the more mysterious and terrifying. I overheard the word 'cancer' for the first time in my life.

CHAPTER 4

Mother

My mother was often ill when I was an infant and she spent much time in bed due to back problems and chronic bronchitis. Many years later, her back problems were discovered to be caused by a rare kidney condition which was, like so many health conditions of that time and place, undiagnosed. She was never able to reconcile herself to island life and to her, Islay, far from being a place of natural richness and beauty, was a kind of prison from which she longed to escape. When she first went to the small shop in Port Askaig for groceries, she heard the few other customers in the shop conversing in the alien tongue of Gaelic and being somewhat prone to paranoia, she assumed that those islanders were judging her, criticising and questioning what she, a complete outsider, was doing here. She never recovered from that initial feeling of rejection and she never returned to that shop on the pier. The chore of shopping passed down the ages of her children who would enter that village store with its wide range of goods, clutching a shopping list which rarely, if ever, varied from week to week. By not attending the shop with the opportunity to meet her neighbours, my mother became even more isolated.

However, she did on some Saturdays go shopping in Bowmore – the island's capital – which, in comparison to Port Askaig, had a range of shops. She always enjoyed a bus trip, even if it was just the ten miles to Bowmore. My parents never learned to drive, not that they could have afforded a car anyway, so travelling by bus was my mother's only means of escape from home with its repetitive and never-ending chores and five demanding children. On the morning of the bus trip, she would dab powder all over her face which gave her a rather ghostly pallor. She would often take me with her and we'd walk down the drive, her with a large shopping bag slung over her arm, and get on the bus at the pier. The bus schedule was tied to the ferry times and the ferry was often late in arriving and departing. Therefore, you couldn't be sure what time the bus would leave and what time it would return. When the bus did leave, I felt a sense of excitement as it made its way up the steep, winding brae with stone walls on either side. In spring, there was the blaze of yellow gorse and further on, I gazed at the brown and black cattle grazing on the lush fields. We passed the primary school, in the small village of Keills, which I was soon to attend for the next seven years of my life. The bus would go under the bridge outside Bridgend which was so low that I felt the need to duck my head and then we were met with the wide expanse of Loch Indaal which almost divides the island into two. Strands of sunlight would appear to dance on the surface of the sea loch and oyster catchers with their starched white shirt fronts stabbing their orange beaks into the sand when the tide was out. On the far side of the loch, I glimpsed the whitewashed houses along the Rhinns.

Finally, we got off the bus on the wide main street of Bowmore which although a small village, to my eyes was a metropolis with its shops and pavements on which people passed to and fro. Over the years, my mother got to know a few fellow shoppers and when talking to them, she would put on what she regarded as her best accent to conceal her native, strong Borders one. However, her best accent involved the adoption of peculiar pronunciations. For example, in front of others and in a desperate attempt to sound posh, she would say *James, get june ute of there* instead of *get down out of there*. Instead of saying *thank you,* she would say *thank o*. When she wasn't making this futile attempt to sound posh, she would revert to her Borders dialect and whenever she was surprised, amused or exasperated by something, she would exclaim: *Heather Joke*. Before she was married, she worked as a maid in large houses owned by those she regarded as her social superiors; she was always attempting to please the *higher ups* and this included most strangers. She had difficulty with any word which contained the letter *a* which she pronounced as *aw*. Her favourite soap powder, *Daz* became *Dawz* and so on. She spent much of her life with soap suds up to her elbows. Her diction was also hampered by the fact that she was only able to wear the top set of dentures and not the bottom one as she felt it too uncomfortable to do so. This lack of a bottom set caused her to drool a little when she was eating. Not only did she feel herself outside the language of Gaelic, she felt herself outside the language of English like many working class Scots.

Above the steep brae of Bowmore, the Round Church gazed down on the scene with an ever watchful eye. A small group of men also stood at a street corner, smoking and watching, as if waiting for something to happen. Their watching made my mother feel uneasy and she would look the other way as she passed them. Although she didn't have much money to spend, she enjoyed browsing in the butcher shop, the bakers and the *Co-op* calling out *thank o* as she left each shop. Very occasionally, we would enter the shoe shop which had the name, *Hodginson* printed above the door in fading paint. I liked the smell of leather as we entered the shop out of the rain – it was usually raining. On those wet days, my mother would take her 'rain mate' out of her handbag, put it over her home permed hair, and tie the strings beneath her chin like a soldier entering into battle.

My favourite part of the shopping trip was our visit to the cafe where we had to climb steep stairs. The cafe had a juke box and I was intrigued to watch the mechanical arm put the record into position and then begin to play. I always had an ice drink which consisted of lemonade and ice-cream. There were often a few men in their teens or twenties in the cafe wearing leather jackets who my mother looked disapprovingly at. When she later discovered that one of those *layabouts* was the boyfriend of her youngest daughter, Muriel, she looked even more disapprovingly at them.

There was often a long wait to get the bus home as it depended on how late the ferry arrived at the other island pier at Port Ellen. I remember standing shivering in a brisk wind off Loch Indaal as we waited and waited to get home. Finally, I would see the bus making its way down the steep brae and climb on board and feel the warmth against my face. I'd be taken once more past the familiar landmarks: the monument on a mound outside Bridgend in memory of the 19th century Celtic scholar, John Francis Campbell, with the river running through the village; the gated drive to Islay House with its woodlands which were carpeted by snowdrops in early spring, their heads nodding in unison in the wind and later the surging waves of bluebells. We passed Ballygrant with its limestone quarry where clouds of dust settled on the leaves of the sycamores after each explosion and then past Keills again with its ancient cemetery and its intricately carved headstones, surrounded by lichened walls. Then the bus began its descent down the steep brae to Port Askaig with its tortuous bends with me clinging on to the seat in front of me, frightened that the brakes of the bus might fail and we would crash through the low wall at the U bend of the brae and the bus would somersault over the high cliff and land on the pier far below. I once overheard someone relate how a motorcyclist had lost control of his bike and had fallen down the cliff and his body had been found smashed to pieces on the pier. Like so many overheard tales of my childhood, I cannot vouch for their factual accuracy but nonetheless they left a deep impression on my mind, and that fear of being driven down that brae, particularly in a bus, remains with me even when I return to the island as an adult. The neat division of time into past and present is a fiction as they are both inextricably bound up with each other. In order to relieve her stress about getting meals ready on time, my mother would always have the kitchen clock set twenty minutes ahead. She lived in that time out of time. Like all of us, she drew some comfort from the illusion that her life lay somewhere ahead of her where she could no longer feel anxious about the present moment and hurt by memories of her past.

CHAPTER 5

Father

That Victorian walled garden was the centre of my father's world. It must have been in a state of neglect when he first arrived and he worked long hours in order to create something beautiful and productive. In the months of spring and summer, he would work seven days each week. He was fortunate in that gardening was his hobby as well as his job. To open the garden door was to step into a world of dazzling colour and scent with the sweet peas a riot of blues, reds, pinks and whites as they clambered up the wire trellises as if driven skyward by their own momentum. The curved petals of the roses ruffled by the soft breezes of summer. The herbaceous border with its phlox, delphiniums and lupins standing to attention with the aid of wooden stakes and oiled twine. The blackcurrant bushes against the back wall revealing their ripened clusters of currants when a breeze lifted their coarse leaves. The branches of the gooseberries arched with the weight of their swollen fruit. The strawberry beds kept beneath black nets to protect them from hungry birds. Sometimes, I'd see a trapped blackbird or thrush flapping its wings frantically as it struggled to release itself from the net and my father would come to release it, removing his pocket knife from his back pocket and cutting the net to free the bird. But there were times when the bird would have already strangled itself before it could be freed and its lifeless body would be thrown over the wall into the rhododendrons.

The greenhouses took up much of my father's time both in summer and winter. In early summer, he would paint the panes of the greenhouses with a green wash in order to shade the plants from strong sunlight. In the top greenhouse, nectarines grew, delicately espaliered along wires. In spring, my father would pollinate the pink blossom with a rabbit's tail bound around the tip of a bamboo cane or he would use a wad of cotton wool instead. He would gently caress the pink flowers, slowly moving the cane up and down and from side to side as if he was conducting an orchestra with a baton. Later he would spray the fantail of nectarines with water, his thumb pressed on the tip of the hose and, in ribbons of sunlight, the spray of water would take on the colours of a rainbow.

Slowly, over the months, the hard, green fruits, those which had not been removed or had fallen on to the soft earth, would swell and then turn a blushing, reddish yellow, patched with cream. As my father gently turned the fruit from the stem to release it, he would hold it in his cupped hand and place it in a wicker trug. As each globed fruit was removed, it would leave its scent trail in the warm, damp air of the greenhouse. In the cool of the potting shed, each gathered nectarine was swaddled with a sheet of tissue paper and placed in a drawer to soften and blush a little longer before it was taken to the Big House for Mr Schroder and his house guests to bite into it with the sweet juice dribbling down their chins, probably not giving a thought to the skill and dedication taken to produce such delights. Those times when he so tenderly cared for the globed fruits, like separate worlds, of the nectarines at Dunlossit and the peaches at Sorn came back to haunt my father's last days in the nursing home in Elgin in which he died.

Down the steps from the top greenhouse, you crossed a paved, patio area where a grapevine spread itself up and along the south facing, whitewashed wall and down slippery stone steps to the bottom greenhouse where the scents of climbing geraniums pervaded the air. On slatted benches, an array of pot plants stood in rows like resplendent soldiers on parade. The mottled leaves of colias brushed against the blowsy heads of begonias; the heads of carnations nodded on thin, wiry stems against the leaves of pelargoniums. The scent of the flowers and wet leaves were mixed with the linseed oil of the wooden frames of the greenhouse and the putty of a recently mended, loose frame of glass. In the winter, there was the added smell of the pink paraffin heater, its blue flames flickering behind its meshed cage which cast ghostly shadows which were mirrored by the differing angles of glass. To test the dryness of each clay flowerpot, my father would tap it with an empty thread reel at the end of a short cane and listen to the sound it made. If it made a dull sound, it meant that the pot was not in need of watering but if it made a ringing sound, it showed that the compost was dry. Listening to him tap each pot was like listening to the playing of a xylophone and those notes have come to echo down the years.

In early spring, my father would spend much time in the potting shed where he would make his own compost with equal parts of loam, leaf mould and sharp sand. The ingredients of the compost would be spread out on the wooden bench like the ingredients of a cake before it was mixed and baked. In order to sterilize the loam, he would fill a rusted pan with it and set it on top of a paraffin heater and steam would rise into the air like steam from boiling potatoes. There is nothing quite like the smell of hot, moist soil which penetrates your nostrils rather like *Vick* rubbed on your chest when you are in bed with a cold. There was the stack of freshly washed clay pots turned upside down on a lower shelf to drain. There was the orange fragments of broken pots on the ribbed, stone floor which would be used for drainage for each whole one.

After a while, I would feel oppressed by the gloom of the potting shed which sunlight never penetrated and I would go down the steps from the top floor of the shed to the lower level where there was a green door which opened out on to a long stretch of grass on which I first learned how to kick a plastic football. Along one side of the grass was a wall on which espaliered apples grew down to the coal shed and along the wall of the garages where more apples were trained, turning a crimson red in early autumn. After the darkness of the potting shed, opening that bottom door was to enter a world of light.

Another of my father's many jobs was ensuring that the boiler which heated the *Big House* was kept going throughout the winter months. The boiler was in a low-ceilinged, cellar-like building below the Big House and sometimes I would go with him down the drive from our house, following the narrow tunnel of light formed by his torch. To enter the boiler room was to enter a warm cave, its walls illumined by the glow of the fire from the smoked glass panel of its door. The room was pervaded by the smell of burning coke and flecks of ash would hang as if suspended in mid-air. When the door was opened by a metal rod curved at the end, there would be a sudden blaze which lit up my father's face and then he would shovel coke from a dark mound and the flames would be dowsed for a time and clouds of smoke would billow until the door was slammed shut.

On some of those evenings, there was no need of a torch to light our way as the moon cast its meshed net over the sea and across the land. The stars formed pearl necklaces across the dome of sky and the trees glowed as if lit from within; the frosted rhododendrons held out their rigid palms like stretched hands at Communion. Sometimes, a cargo boat passed slowly along the Sound with its long, lit deck and I heard the throb, throb, of its engine echoing through the frozen air.

Chapter 6

Cigarette Smoke and Milk Cans

The owner of Dunlossit Estate was the merchant banker, Helmut Schroder, who to my childish eyes seemed such an austere and distant figure. He would come up from London each summer, and often in the deer stalking season in autumn, with his family and his entourage of servants to occupy the *Big House* for months. His arrival altered the atmosphere of the estate and the mood of the scores of islanders who lived and worked on it whether in the forestry, the limestone quarry, or as gamekeepers, beaters or tenant farmers. For those few months in the summer, Dunlossit lost its air of peace and sleepiness and *Land Rovers* and cars would clatter across the cattle grid at the Gate Lodge and raise dust from the limestone drive or splash through the gathered puddles. My father would spend even more time mowing the front and back lawns, creating stripes which were lit up by sun and darkened when the clouds moved across them. It was usually in the afternoons that the grass was mowed in order to avoid awakening the still sleeping guests in the Big House. My father would spend hours on summer mornings ensuring that the mowers were in full working order: sharpening and adjusting the blades, checking that the blend of petrol and oil was correct and so on. There was nowhere on the island to have motor mowers serviced so an estate gardener had to be something of a mechanic, along with so much else. Before the great arrival, my father and his under-gardener, Dan Macaulay, would spend much of the day edging the grass verges all along the drive and hoeing the weeds which grew so quickly along its sides in the mild, often wet summers.

large, walk-in fridge where the dead birds were hung by the neck like rows of the executed.

The gamekeeper often swore in a loud voice and I would hear his expletives echo from that tiled room, all the words which were forbidden for children to repeat. He seemed to have not much regard for the suffering of the slaughtered birds and mammals: the pheasants, woodcock, snipe, ducks, grouse, rabbits, hares and deer now riddled with lead pellets. I recall once that he removed the bladder of a stag and gave it to my brother and me, saying that it would make an ideal football if we inflated it. His assistant gamekeeper was no less uncaring of animals and he had a particular dislike of cats. There were several wild, or simply abandoned cats, who roamed the estate forests and whenever he was able to catch one, he would swing the bewildered creature by the tail around his head like a hammer thrower at the Highland Games; letting it go, with the poor creature flying through the air and its landing would not always have been soft. However, it is important to add that all of the island gamekeepers had a vital role to play in keeping down the numbers of red deer, as failing to do so would lead to the slow starvation of the weaker animals.

My father used to warn us to be careful when we walked along the shore below our house as the gamekeepers set powerful traps between the rocks in order to kill otters who were regarded at that time as vermin. This attitude to this beautiful animal was shared by my father and on one shocking occasion, he discovered an otter in the garage where he kept his motor mowers and he killed it by hitting it across the nose with a spade. He hit the struggling otter again and again and after its sleek body lay lifeless on the oil-soaked concrete floor of the garage, my father expressed his admiration for the fight it had put up.

When our pet collie called Dawn had a litter of pups, my father would put them into a hessian sack, along with a couple of boulders, then throw the sack into the sea at the end of the Wee Pier below our house. The drowning of puppies and kittens was standard practice among the islanders. I think the established church had some influence in this contempt for animal life with its teaching of man's *dominion over the fish of the sea, and over the fowl of the air, and over the cattle, and over all the earth, and over every creeping thing that creepeth upon the earth.*

Of course, if this attitude to the animal kingdom did not exist, there would have been no such large private estates in the Highlands and Islands like Dunlossit which were bought and largely maintained for the slaughter of wild, or not so wild, birds and animals. The pheasants which were reared by hand were closer to being pets than wild animals. Helmut Schroder had a love of shooting and he employed his gamekeepers to provide enough game – the word is revealing – for he and his wealthy guests to shoot. The lochs and the rivers on the estate were used to provide brown trout and salmon to catch with slim, elegant rods with intricately tied flies. There is so much skill and knowledge required in the pursuit of slaughter.

Gamekeepers and farmers would trap, shoot and poison any bird or mammal which was often arbitrarily classed as vermin. The estate gamekeepers were under pressure to provide ideal conditions for the shooting parties which arrived from the mainland each year as guests of the landowners just as my father was under pressure to provide flowers, fruit and vegetables for the Big House. My brother, George and I were influenced by this prevailing disregard for the welfare of animals and it gave rise to the most shameful incident of my childhood.

There was a farmer who lived near Keills who, even by island standards, was notorious for his disregard for the welfare of his sheep. His flock would wander all over Dunlossit Estate with their dirty fleece hanging off their backs, their exposed flesh eaten and reddened with maggots and diseases. It never seemed to occur to anyone to report this farmer for neglect, it was, like so many aspects of life on the island, simply accepted. There was one sheep which was in a sorry state which George and I, along with two other children, came across as it made its way over the sloping back lawn of the Big House. We herded the limping sheep with its dragging fleece up the lawn and down the slippery steps hedged by wild garlic. Whenever the sheep stopped and turned to us with her bewildered, pleading eyes, we would throw stones at her which we had gathered from the drive. The sheep slithered down to the bottom of the steps and instead of making her way on to the Wee Pier, she turned left and tried to take refuge beneath an arch of rock, like a cave. The sheep could go no further and she lay down exhausted. We showed no mercy and went on throwing stones at her and she lay there motionless with her head resting on the fallen rocks, her eyes blank. I cannot be certain if she was dead or if she lay for hours suffering. All I know is that when I came back the next day, I saw quite clearly that she was dead. The only movement was made by the wind lifting and letting fall her ragged fleece.

The memory of that terrible event has remained deeply ingrained within me. I came to shun that cave for fear that I would be met with the accusing eyes of her ghost. Years later, I did return to that arch of rock and the image of the tormented sheep flooded into my mind. I remember, above all, her sad, frightened eyes as if pleading for pity which we boys were incapable of giving. That act revealed to me that violence and the perverse delight in inflicting needless suffering on some vulnerable being was as much a part of me, as of all those one reads about in the daily news. Despite all the advances in science and technology, the world is just as violent a place as it ever has been throughout history. I am not suggesting that killing a sheep is of the same order as killing a human but nonetheless, the instinct to inflict pain for no good reason except to give oneself a momentary feeling of power is not so far removed as one might like to think.

CHAPTER 8

The Wee Room with Wide Windows

My enclosed infant life at Dunlossit came to an end one morning at the end of August when I started school. I remember how loudly the birds sang from the trees as I walked with my mother and brother down the drive, past the Big House with the Union Jack fluttering on the flagpole as if waving me goodbye. My mother turned back at the lodge and George and I walked across the cattle grid, up the steep brae and past Caol Ila road end with the coconut scent of gorse bushes carried by a breeze. Finally, after a mile or so, we reached Keills Primary. My first day at school coincided with the opening of the new school but first, I was taken to the old school and to a room with a fireplace and old, worm-eaten wooden desks with the names of past pupils carved by penknives and stained by ink. I remember being handed a small slate and a piece of chalk and not knowing what I was supposed to do with them and how frightened and bewildered I felt. It was as if I had been set down in an alien land where they did things differently. Although there must have been less than thirty pupils in the school and only two teachers, I had no experience of being among so many people. I found myself longing to return to my solitary pursuits and daydreams.

I was then taken to the new school which was only some thirty yards away across the playground with its long grass. The new school was divided into the Wee Room and the Big Room. The Wee Room was for classes Primary 1, 2 and 3 and the Big Room was for classes 4, 5, 6 and 7. My brother was in the third row at the far side of the Wee Room, his desk closest to the wide side window. After the gloom and bare walls of the old school, I was struck by the brightness of the Wee Room with its pictures on the walls and its wide windows. From one window, you could look down across the fields and to the woodlands of Dunlossit, the sight of which gave me some comfort. It seemed so close and yet a world away. Beyond the lines of trees, I could glimpse the Sound and on the other side, the scoured, brown slopes of Jura.

When I turned my head to look through the side window, I looked out on the playing field which was enclosed by drystane walls on which hooded crows would perch from time to time, with their staring, accusing eyes, their black tail feathers with a stray strand of sun lighting the sheen of their breasts. Later in the morning, I caught a glimpse of an old man slowly swinging his scythe through the long grass at the bottom of the playground and sometimes bending down to sharpen the blade with a curved, narrow stone.

I was shown to a small, varnished desk with a round hole for an ink well on the ledge. When you raised the lid of the desk, the hinges complained a little. I had never seen a desk before. There must have been a dozen or so desks in the room and they were arranged in three rows: the first row nearest the door was for Primary 1, the second row for Primary 2 and the third row for Primary 3. Over the three years you spent in this room, you gradually moved across it to the side window which looked out on the playing field and the stone wall with its observing crows.

At 11am I heard the ringing of a bell which seemed to come from the Big Room and we were told that it was time for milk and I followed the class in single file to the dining-room where I was handed a beaker of milk which I struggled to drink in my nervous condition but I felt that I had to finish it. After the ordeal of the milk, I remember following the others out of the back door of the school which led to a shelter and to the playground where some of the older and bigger children kicked a ball around. My father had taught me how to kick a ball and I enjoyed doing so but I felt much too daunted to join in the game on my first day. Behind the fence, brown cattle grazed, their tails swinging like pendulums to disperse the flies. The field was patchworked by cow pats which had dried and crusted in the sun. Looking up, I saw the clouds altering their patterns in the sky. I longed for this day to end and return to all that I was most familiar with at home. Although I was only a mile or so from home, the distance seemed immeasurable.

For an infant, time appears as an eternal present and after an age, the bell rang for lunchtime and we filed again into the dining-room and I took my place at the small table. I forced myself to swallow the food which was set in front of me although each mouthful made me feel sick. After the trauma of lunch, I stood in the shelter watching the other children play.

Somehow, 3pm at last arrived and the bell for release was sounded and George and I, along with the infants from Caol Ila, made our way along the road to Port Askaig and to home. This was to be my routine for the next seven years of my life, with a few variations. I moved one row across the Wee Room each year until my desk was at the back of the row closest to the side window and I could gaze out at the crows shifting their claws on the drystane wall and watch the long grass move in the wind and daydream of being somewhere else. As I look back now, I long to be back at that desk gazing out of the wide window when the future was filled with so many possibilities, however vague. What I did not know as a child is that the longing to be someone else and to be somewhere else remains throughout one's life. The imagined future never comes.

After three years in that Wee Room with colourful pictures on the walls, I made one of the biggest steps in my life in moving a few yards next door to enter the fearful world of the Big Room in which the headmaster, Donald MacKechnie, whose nickname was *Squeak* because when he was reduced to anger, as he often was, his voice took on the pitch of an angry mouse. In the safety of the Wee Room, I would, from time to time, hear his voice echo through the wall. I rather dreaded my future promotion to that room next door. I now think of that saying by the Chinese philosopher, Lao Tzu: *The journey of a thousand miles begins with one step.* I was to spend the next four years in that Big Room, moving across the rows until I again found myself sitting at a desk closest to the side window where my dreams and longings to be someone and somewhere else intensified.

Although it took me a long time to come to terms with going to school, there were some moments of happiness. One of my favourite activities in the Wee Room was in those afternoons when the teacher would read us a story. I always found the teacher, Mrs Fisher a rather forbidding lady who tended to favour some pupils above others and I resented the fact that I certainly wasn't one of her favoured ones. However, there was a soothing sound to her voice as she read of worlds which were not my own. Just as one of my earliest memories of being blissfully happy was sitting at the card table playing with small plastic farm animals, my favourite stories were of farms with hens pecking stray sheaves of corn in the farmyard; cattle gently lowing; sheep with fleeces dazzling in the sunlight – in those stories it was an eternal sunlit summer – geese and ducks splashing in ponds and children laughing as they slid down hayricks. The farmer would invariably have the surname of Giles and his wife with her rosy cheeks would be forever smiling. As she read, the teacher would hold up the book so that we could gaze on the brightly coloured illustrations. Although I had visited the estate farm at Keills a few times to collect the milk, with its mud and clutter and air of neglect, it bore little resemblance to the farms in the story books. It was because the stories I listened to with their ever cheerful and polite Mummy and Daddy who never shouted at each other or their children and who never became bored and frustrated by the drudgery of their days were so unlike the world I inhabited that they appealed to me so much.

CHAPTER 9

The Big House

Those in the Wee Room were allowed to leave an hour earlier than those in the Big Room and when George had graduated to the Big Room, he had to remain at school until 4pm and I would walk home with the infants from Caol Ila at 3pm. Some afternoons in summer, when it was dry, my mother would follow the faint footpath over the hill from the clearing in the woodland above our house to meet me at Caol Ila road end. Once she was chased by an escaped bull which had forced its way through the rickety fence. There was a caravan parked near the gate which led to the road and the bull chased my mother round and round the caravan. Perhaps my mother had been wearing her garishly flowered, cross your heart apron which she rarely took off and this unsettled the bull. My mother was a stout woman and I had never seen her run before – or since – and as I stood leaning on the safe side of the gate, I was rather impressed by the speed she maintained as she repeated her circuits of the caravan. After a while, the bull gave up the chase, perhaps through boredom, and he wandered off, shaking his head as he went as if in disbelief and my mother collapsed on to a boulder, gasping for breath. Incidents such as those made her dislike island life still more. I can't recall her walking over the hill to meet me from school again.

Although my mother had lived nearly all her life in the countryside, she was never a country lover and would have been happier living close to shops and hairdressers and other amenities. She longed to live in a warm house with fitted carpets and central heating but instead her husband led her to one cold, damp estate house after another with floors on which the linoleum would lift and wrinkle in the sudden draughts which made their way beneath the gaps in the outer doors where the only source of heat was often a stubborn coal fire in the grate which also heated the oven to an indeterminate temperature. This trauma with the bull left a lasting impression on her and it confirmed her belief that she had landed in an alien world where many people spoke a language which might as well have been Cantonese as Gaelic.

As the wife of the gardener, my mother was expected to work in the Big House during the summer season when Mr Schroder brought his family and friends to Islay. Later, each of my sisters would also serve in the Big House. Of course, such wealthy people were not able to fend for themselves and a legion of servants would be brought along to attend to the many demands of their superiors. There would be a cook, a butler, waitresses, house maids, pantry maids and kitchen maids, a chauffeur and so on. The arrival of all those strangers brought an element of excitement as it broke the routine of our lives. The House staff were mostly from the London area which I, who did not set foot off the island for the first seven years of my life, regarded as a strange and far distant land where crowds jostled against each other in the struggle for existence. It seemed extraordinary to me that people could live with such a lack of space. I had seen photographs of cities in books and they reminded me of the ant hills I had seen in the walled garden. The Cockney accents of some of the staff stood out on an island of soft, lilting voices.

Some of the staff seemed to me to be rather surreal people, more akin to characters in *Oliver Twist*. There was the tall butler, appropriately called, Mr Long, brim-full of an awareness of his own grandeur, who wore a black jacket with immaculately pressed trousers, which had narrow, grey stripes and polished shoes which mirrored his self-satisfied face. His wife regarded herself as the equal to any aristocrat and her face was always skilfully powdered and painted.

There was the chauffeur who went to the pub in Port Askaig on his nights off and who got drunk one Saturday night and *borrowed* the estate *Land Rover* which he drove along the back drive past the Lily Loch and Loch Allan, accompanied by a local lady with a reputation for loose morals. This woman who was the mother of a girl around my own age had a remarkable cheerfulness and wore an almost constant smile on her face as if she had found the secret of eternal happiness. Her husband had left her so she did not have to live the cripplingly respectable life of the married woman who was constantly concerned about what her neighbours and the minister might say. People were critical of her behind her back but she had the enviable ability to ignore the gossip which surrounded her. This disapproving gossip only increased when the chauffeur she was with crashed the *Land Rover* against a tree and came close to landing it in Ballygrant Loch which would no doubt have disturbed the resident swans. There was much whispering about this incident by my parents – my mother had the curious ability to whisper more loudly than when she talked normally so keeping secrets was not her strongest point – and by others on the estate. This chauffeur was packed off back to London shortly after his night-time adventure and his replacement duly arrived, no doubt bewildered to find himself on an island he had probably never even heard of.

There was the devout Roman Catholic cook – like many islanders I had never come across anyone who possessed such an exotic, if rather suspicious faith. This highly strung lady who wore a small, gold cross around her neck, was prone to stress and she would shout at the kitchen staff or anyone within earshot. Once, in her anger she threw a cabbage, presumably grown by my father, at a maid which blackened her eye. After such a violent outburst, she dissolved in floods of tears and asked forgiveness as though in the confessional box. She was not really suited to life in a house which was like a pressure cooker whose lid could blow off at any moment. Most of the *servants*, as no doubt some of the more snobbish guests would have referred to them, lived in the Big House in a separate wing in which the bedrooms were far less grand than those of the Schroders and their guests and there was little opportunity to escape from each other. There were also the stresses of looking after the many guests, each with his or her own demanding ways. The staff worked long hours and it was late in the evening before they could retire after dinner had been served and the clearing and washing up was done. At the end of each long day, the staff would retire to the small downstairs parlour and complain about and mock their *superiors*: the way they ate at the dining table with the blood from grouse, cooked rare, dribbling down their chins; the silly remarks they made; the clandestine affairs, real or imagined, which were carried on behind the wife or husband's back and so on. Many years later, I was struck by WM Thackeray's remark that *no man is a hero to his valet* and going by what my sisters told me about their experiences of working at Dunlossit House, that was certainly the case. It is those who serve the aristocracy who are in the best position to perceive that their pettiness, vanities and jealousies are no different from our own.

My father would invite members of the staff up to our house for a drink from time to time and I think that they appreciated a brief escape from their restricted lives in the Big House where their every move was observed and commented upon. They would talk about their lives in a world which seemed so far removed from our own. Most missed the life of the city with all its shops and entertainments but a few came to appreciate the beauty and spaciousness of the island. My mother was much less sociable than my father, she could rarely overcome her suspicion of strangers. It was as if she did not want anyone prying into the intimate parts of her life. Perhaps it was partly because her sister, Nell had borne children out of wedlock which was seen as such a shameful act in an age when moral respectability was everything. *You may be poor but at least you had your good name.* However, my mother did come to rather like or at least tolerate the cabbage throwing cook who would visit for a cup of tea on occasion. Perhaps she recognized a fellow sufferer in this easily stressed, volatile lady who so often bemoaned her lot in life and longed for something better. My mother would often say that she was *hattered to daith* meaning that her stress levels were even higher than usual. If she could not get her washing dry on a Monday or her husband was even later than normal coming in for his dinner or if she was rushing to be in time to catch the bus to Bowmore, she would be *hattered to daith*. The cook's Catholic faith would have been a source of suspicion to my mother but she did not share the deep-seated bigotry of my father which had been bred into him with his mother's milk. My mother's Borders childhood saved her from the prejudices which were endemic in my father's childhood on the outskirts of Glasgow with its Orange Lodges and flag waving marches.

This group of strangers from a strange land who disrupted the peace of Dunlossit at least twice each year was something which, on the whole, we welcomed as it brought colour and entertainment into our lives and variety to the sameness of our days. I suppose that it had the effect similar to that of a travelling circus which sets up in a field outside a small town with its ringmaster, acrobats, clowns and bearded ladies. It introduced me to a cast of characters I would not otherwise have met and it revealed to me that there were as many ways of perceiving the world as there are people.

CHAPTER 10

The Storm

I was seven before I ever set foot on the mainland which was to me only a place of myth and rumour. Against all the odds, my mother had at last persuaded her husband to take us on a family holiday. Needless to say, her powers of persuasion did not extend to making my father go away in summer with greenhouses to attend to, grass to mow, fruit and vegetables to harvest, flowers to cut and so on and so on. I doubt if my father ever had a summer holiday in his entire working life. It was autumn before we could leave, with its storms which came so close to costing us our lives. The excitable, devout Catholic cook happened to sail on the same two ferries as ourselves and I came to be glad of her fervent prayers.

As with many working class families at that time, our holiday was to be spent not in a boarding house or in a hotel or in a rented cottage but involved uncomfortable stays with relatives on the *mainland*, that mysterious world I had never seen but had vaguely imagined. On that Saturday morning in autumn with the sky a threatening, metallic grey, we boarded the *Lochiel* at Port Askaig and set sail for the *mainland*. When the ferry called in at Jura and Gigha, I was struck by the small crowd of people who had congregated on the pier as if the arrival of the boat was the social highlight of their day. Some passengers got off and some boarded and they stood on the deck and frantically waved to those who were left behind; the wake left by the ferry widening and fading as it moved out of the shelter of the harbour.

Someone once told my mother that seasickness might be avoided if she sat on a newspaper and this advice she followed on her all too few voyages away from Islay. Her adviser did not state if it mattered what newspaper was used for this purpose but as *The Daily Express, The Oban Times and The Sunday Post* – which arrived every Tuesday – were the newspapers we purchased, it must have been one of those. My father did get the *Gardeners' Chronicle* but the pages would have been too small for my mother's substantial bottom and she may have slipped off the shiny illustrations and rolled along the sloping deck, unable to get back up. The newspapers also served their purpose as toilet paper when cut into small squares when the *Izal* ran out. The *Gardeners' Chronicle* would also have been unsuitable for this purpose. My mother's continued adherence to sitting on newspaper, whatever its benefits, did little to alleviate her terror of the sea but it seemed to provide a small element of reassurance. The *Lochiel* was totally unsuited to the stormy crossings to and from Islay in the autumn and winter and it tossed like a cork on the rising and falling of the waves. For passengers it was like being on a roller coaster. My mother felt it wiser to stay on the lower deck and avoid, at all costs, looking through the streaming portholes at the sea. She and the Catholic cook sat beside each other, as if for solace.

I, on the other hand, stood on the deck beside my father and George, holding on to the rusted railings and looking at the loved, familiar landmarks of my world from a different perspective: there was the lifeboat station; the Wee Pier where we fished for saithe, considered to be inedible; the small lighthouse with its jetty sloping down to the sea; the turbine house whitewashed beneath an arch of trees and, finally, MacArthur's Head lighthouse perched on a high rock, guarding the Sound of Islay. I watched the centre of my world slowly dissolve from my sight.

After some three hours, we reached the safety of the sheltered sea loch of West Loch Tarbert on the Kintyre peninsula. On one side, I saw cattle standing on the shore with their heads bowed. The ferry reversed into the pier, and we struggled down the narrow gangway with our suitcases and boarded a bus which would take us to East Loch Tarbert where, to my mother's alarm, we would board another ferry which would take us to Gourock, through the Kyles of Bute. On this sailing, my mother's fears proved to be justified as the ferry, the *Loch Fyne*, came very close to capsizing in a storm and if it had done so, we would almost certainly have drowned. We were later informed that the winds reached Storm Force 11.

As we boarded this second ferry, the wind began to rise and I felt the salt spray sting my face. Normally, the ferry would not have sailed if there was a forecast of dangerous winds but this being Saturday, the captain and his crew who came mostly from the Glasgow area were keen to get home for the weekend so they decided to take a risk: after all, the Kyles of Bute would be sheltered from the worst of the winds. However, we were not far out from the horseshoe harbour of Tarbert when the ferry began to rock from side to side and to dip and rise in the onrush of foaming waves. The white horses began to gallop faster and faster. In the more exposed parts of the sea, the waves began to flood over the top deck of the ship and in the enclosed lower deck in which my mother and the cook sat, the salt water was rising above their ankles. My father, George and I struggled down the stairs, clutching the handrails, as the ship swayed and dipped violently, to join them.

There we sat for a seemingly endless period of time in increasing terror. If the chairs on which we sat had not been fixed to the floor, we would all have been driven across the low-ceilinged cabin which now took on the confined dimensions of a coffin, crashing into each other as if on a dodgem track. The cook murmured prayers ceaselessly, beseeching God to save us. For some reason, I pretended to sleep with my head hidden in my arm laid across the back of the chair as if I felt the need to conceal my terror. I wondered what it would feel like to drown, to feel the breath and the life choked out of me. I prayed inwardly, pleading with God to let me live, to let myself and my family set foot on land once more, to be allowed time to fulfil my vague dreams of the future: those daydreams I had as I sat at my desk in the Wee Room at Keills, gazing out of the side window at my desk on the third row which I had at last reached. My silent prayers were interrupted by the voice of a stranger who told my mother that her handbag, which was so precious to her, was floating away in the ever-deepening water in the lounge and the tearful voice of my mother replying: *I winna be needin' that where am goin'*. In her fear and despair, she no longer felt the need to put on what she regarded as her posh voice in the presence of strangers.

Her words brought home still more forcefully, that I was soon to be swallowed whole by the icy waves along with the precious handbag. It was in this bag, which my mother clutched over her arm like a comfort blanket whenever she went anywhere, that she kept her comb, her purse, her rain mate, her circular tin of powder which she dabbed on her face and which gave her a curious ghostly appearance to my childish eyes and the ferry tickets. All I could do was go on silently and fervently praying to a God whose presence I kept inside my mind. I had heard a little about Christianity in school and we sang hymns in class. On rare sunlit mornings, we would sing:

> *All things bright and beautiful*
> *All creatures great and small*
> *All things wise and wonderful*
> *T'was God that made them all.*

I had also seen depictions of Christ in an illustrated Bible with His sad, kind, downward gaze. However, I felt that the God to whom I prayed was not much influenced by what I had been taught, but a presence who had been with me from the beginning. God was the deepest aspect of myself and despite the many doubts and questions which adulthood has brought, that sense of some mysterious inner presence has remained.

Having given up almost all hope of survival, slowly, almost imperceptibly, the rocking of the ship became less violent, the dips into the waves became less steep. The sea water around our feet became less deep as if on the rowing boat on Loch Allen when we had reached the shallower water close to the shore. My father led myself and George upstairs and on to the open deck and we saw the harbour lights of Gourock dispersing the autumnal darkness. These were the lights of safety. As the ferry moved closer and closer to the lit fingers of the pier which reached out towards us like a beckoning hand, I saw the slate grey of naval ships docked with their portal holes casting circles of light on the sea. With the street lamps and the lights of pubs and shops and restaurants of the town, I had never seen such an array of differently coloured lights except on the tree which stood in the hall of our house each Christmas.

I remember that after we lugged our dripping bags and suitcases down the gangway at Gourock and felt the solid pier beneath our feet, my father went into a garishly lighted bar and asked a group of men who sat holding pints of frothy beer at a table, when the next bus to Kilmacolm would arrive. I was struck by the calmness and indifference of the people my father talked to but of course they had no way of knowing that we had come so close to death. In my childhood egotism, I had expected a sort of fanfare as we reached the safety of land against all the odds but the world went on with its own affairs regardless. As we boarded our separate buses, we said goodbye to the cook – it's strange that I cannot remember her name as her fervent prayers left an indelible imprint on my mind on my first journey away from Islay. That traumatic experience left me with the impression that leaving the island, even for a short period, was to court danger. For the first time in my life, I sat on the top deck of a double decker bus as it made its way through a bewildering sea of traffic. I found the noise and the flashing lights of traffic quite overwhelming. We were heading towards the place of my father's childhood and youth but all I wanted to do was to go back home to the only place in which I felt safe.

CHAPTER II

Father's Homecoming

It was late in the evening, well past my bedtime, when we arrived at my grandmother's flat in the tenement building in Kilmacolm which had become a dormer town for the many commuters to Glasgow. I had never met my grandmother before but I had heard a little about her. She was a MacInnes who grew up in the Dunvegan area on the Isle of Skye where her parents had a croft. She was a very small, wiry lady with a face lined like the hills depicted on an ordnance survey map I had once been shown in school. I cannot be sure of her precise age when I met her, all I knew was that she was ancient, so old that after a time they stopped counting. She had lost her husband, Alexander, several years before. I had never met him and all I knew about him was that whenever he had an egg for tea, he would give my father the top of it. As a child, my father did not have the privilege of having a whole egg to himself. This tale remained in my mind as it represented a degree of poverty that I knew little of in my own childhood although we were a long way from being affluent. I expect that the lack of protein in my father's childhood diet explained his low stature and slightly bowed legs. I found my grandmother rather frightening and I said little to her and I have no recollection of what she said to me. I can't recall the precise sleeping arrangements in that small, cramped flat, but I remember that the bed I slept in appeared to keep swaying and rising and falling like the ferry. In my dreams, I relived the storm as if unable to fully grasp that I was now on dry land.

My father's middle-aged brother, my Uncle Jack, still lived with his mother who treated him in a rather domineering manner and he acted

she kissed me goodbye. We got a bus into the bedlam that was Glasgow – no doubt the bus driver was named Jack. At Queen Street Station, I boarded a train for the very first time and in Edinburgh, I boarded my second train; this time a steam train on the Waverley Line to Carlisle but we were not venturing into the strange land of England but to a hamlet in the Borders where my mother's father lived, my grandfather James Knox after whom I was named. Having endured my father's return 'home', I now had to endure my mother's homecoming.

CHAPTER 12

Mother's Homecoming

The train gasped and puffed its way through the Borders landscape, along steep sided valleys grazed by sheep and the high, grey houses of isolated hill farms. I sat in the carriage of the corridor train and listened to the drowsy rhythm of the engine and saw the flecks of ash through the grimy window. My mother told me that as a child she thought that the sound of the steam engine as it struggled up the steep inclines was saying over and over again: *I canna dae it, I hae to dae it, I canna dae it, I hae to dae it.* I later came to think that those repeated words were rather like her life in that there was much which she had to endure. She had a difficult, moody father, who I was about to meet for the first time. She had endured years of drudgery, years which began soon after she left school at the age of fourteen, working as a maid in large houses, undertaking a whole range of jobs in order to make the lives of her gentrified employers more comfortable, no matter what discomforts she herself had to put up with.

It was when she was *in service* in a country house in the Borders that she met my father. They married and had their first child, Isabel. When my mother gave birth to her second child, Catherine, her husband was still in the army, having fought in France in the Second World War. She was not allowed to have two children in the place in which she lived and worked and as a result of that, Catherine was sent to live miles away with an aunt who lived in the town of Workington, across the border, in Cumbria. There is no knowing what lingering feelings of rejection this might have left in the mind of the banished child.

My mother's brother, James, the uncle I never met, was killed in the Second World War. On the scroll his grieving parents received after his death, it is written that he *gave his life to save mankind from tyranny.* However, tyranny was much closer to home. In the year 1900, it was estimated that one working age adult in every three in Britain worked *in service* and although the aftermath of the First World War brought many changes, the life of those *in service* changed painfully slowly.

When my father left the army, he was keen to return to live in Kilmacolm and perhaps obtain a job in the parks department but the prospect of living amid her husband's odd assortment of relatives was too depressing a prospect for my mother. My father obtained a gardening job at Ballindalloch Castle in Banffshire, in north-east Scotland, where they endured some bitter winters in a rather primitive damp and draughty estate house. They somehow survived the ferocious winter of 1947 when severe frost and deep snow lay for month after month. To add to their burden of making ends meet, their third child, Muriel was born. With no transport of their own and far from buses, trains and shops or amenities of any kind, life must have been harsh. From Ballindalloch, they moved to Kilmelford, in Argyll with all its rain and further isolation but where the winters were at least less harsh and the town of Oban could be reached by a regular bus service. On Melfort estate, their fourth child, George was born. My conception at Melfort was the final straw which was to lead to the move to the still more inaccessible destination of Islay which could only be reached by the sea crossing which my mother so much dreaded and which only a few days earlier had come so close to costing her life. There was a small airport on Islay but the fare was way beyond a family of seven whose only income was my father's wage. Anyway, my mother would have found flying almost as terrifying as sailing and never had and never would step on to an aeroplane.

As well as the poverty and isolation, my mother also had to endure two chronic conditions: lumbago and bronchitis. The only relief from her back pain was to swallow codeine tablets and to sit on an armchair with a hot water bottle at her back. I expect she developed something of an addiction to codeine which was more freely available than it is today. Her illnesses and her feelings of resentment towards my father for dragging her to one God forsaken place to another made her bad tempered and unreasonable and she relieved her anger, from time to time, on her two eldest children, Isabel and Catherine. Muriel was always treated as a law unto herself and beyond redemption. As my mother got older, she became, if not more mellow, then more resigned and George and I were spared the worst of her temper.

How excited she must have felt as the train chugged its way closer and closer to her childhood home after so many years of exile. The very names of the stations we stopped at must have brought back youthful memories: Galashiels, Melrose, Hawick – the town in which she was born, with its row of woollen mills – Riccarton Junction and, finally, the small station of Steele Road above the row of railwayman's cottages where her father still lived in his retirement from a lifetime of work on the Waverley Line.

Finally, the train stopped at Steele Road, the huffing and puffing momentarily silenced. My parents lugged their suitcases, stained with salt water from the ferry crossing to Gourock, and stepped down on to the platform of this small, remote station. In the distance, I glanced at the range of brown, brooding hills, so different to the Paps of Jura. We followed a footpath down to the row of cottages and through a back garden and found my grandfather and his daughter who I was told was my Aunt Nell. My grandfather was a small, stocky man with a whitish beard. His face looked stern and unfriendly. I had overheard my father, out of earshot of my mother, describe his father-in-law as a *moaning old bugger* and also heard dark whisperings of his daughter, my Auntie Nell, bearing children even though she never married. Whatever the truth about my aunt, I liked her kind face. She lived in a cottage next door to her father and attended to his needs after the maternal grandmother I had also never met had died.

The next day, George and I went out to play on our own and as we walked along the narrow street that divided the two rows of cottages, I came across strangely small, colourful hens in one of the back gardens. A man was throwing fantails of grain, as if casting seed, on the muddy ground. He smiled at us and asked who we were and where we had come from. To my surprise, he had never heard of Islay. How could anyone not have heard of

Islay? He told us that those peculiar dwarf hens were called bantams and he showed us the tiny egg which he held in his hand. After the adventure of the bantams, we turned to go back to the house in which we had spent the night and found that we could not tell which one it was. As far as I recall, the cottages were identical and not numbered and even if they were, we could not remember the number of our grandfather's. A sense of panic set in, we felt lost in a strange land and we walked up and down the rows becoming so disorientated that we were no longer certain even which side of the road the cottage was on. Like my mother, I was born with little sense of direction, it was as if my inner compass had been damaged at birth. I remember that tears came to my eyes which I tried to conceal. It's strange but I cannot recall how we eventually succeeded in finding our way back to our grandfather's cottage where our parents were, whether it was my Auntie Nell who came to our aid or if we were saved by the kindness of a stranger but that experience of feeling completely lost has remained with me.

My grandfather smoked a pipe and I liked the way in which the rings of smoke rose slowly into the air in the small living-room in which he sat in an armchair like a throne. I also liked the scent of the tobacco which pervaded the room. There was a clock which loudly ticked off the seconds in the long periods of silence between snatches of conversation between my parents and himself. I expect the clock was a retirement present from the railways. A clock seemed to be a common retirement present at that time which seems ironic as when in retirement, time was less important except to measure out the remaining days of the recipient's life when time would seem to move faster and faster. I wondered what my grandfather thought of in those periods of silence as he puffed away at his pipe with brief streams of sunlight filtering through the net curtains in those autumn afternoons when the leaves fell unhurriedly from the beech trees.

If I was vague about my paternal uncles and aunts in Kilmacolm and its surrounding towns, I was even vaguer about my maternal uncles and aunts in the Borders. I did meet briefly, an Uncle Rob, an Uncle Will, an Aunt Alice and so on but my mother's relations seemed so complex and confusing, partly since my grandfather's first wife had died young and that he had re-married and had more children and that his daughter, Nell had borne children who were not acknowledged as her children and so on. All families are complex but some are more complex than others and with the egotism of childhood, I didn't spend time trying to unravel the bewildering strands.

In the days in which we stayed at Steele Road, I only once remember my grandfather leaving his house, even though he was perfectly capable of walking. My parents with George and me had gone for a walk along some deserted road and on the way back, I saw my grandfather slowly coming towards us. As I found his presence rather oppressive, I had mixed feelings about him joining us in my time of relative freedom. I later felt guilty about those feelings as that was my last memory of the man I was named after, as I don't remember him at our leave-taking the next day and I never saw him again. All I really remember on the morning we left, was that my Auntie Nell pressed a coin in my hand and said: *There's a penny for you.* When I opened my hand, I saw a shiny half-crown which was five times my weekly pocket money. With this coin I could buy five *Mars Bars* or ten bars of *McCowan's Highland Toffee*. Although I had never experienced such wealth before, I was puzzled why she should have referred to the coin as a penny. There was no possibility that he, my grandfather would ever come to Islay, the journey, the sea crossing would be far beyond his waning powers of endurance. Although he worked all his life on the railways, like so many working class people of his time, he was never much of a traveller. Like my mother, I doubt if he had ever travelled further south than Carlisle and that is a journey he may only have taken once or twice in his life. I don't suppose that he had ever set foot on a ship of any kind. Some years later, I was told that he had died and because of the expense, the distance and the dreaded ferry crossings, my mother was unable to attend her father's funeral which must have increased her resentment at her enforced imprisonment on Islay – an imprisonment caused by my conception. Many, many years later, my wife, Ann and I visited Steele Road and I was struck by the beauty of the setting of this hamlet which looked across to the russet browns of the Cheviot Hills. It was September and the leaves of the trees were already tinged with oranges and yellows. The Waverley Line had been one of the many victims of the Beeching cuts in the 1960s and the long disused station had been overtaken by tall weeds and brambles but, when I looked closely, I could see the broken concrete of the platform on which I had stepped on to at the age of seven with a fear of who and what I might encounter on my mother's homecoming.

In the nearby village of Newcastleton which my mother always referred to as *The Holm*, we searched out a cousin of mine, Irene, who apparently, I had once met when I was in my early teens, and she told me where my grandfather had been buried. We drove up to a graveyard which was set on a high hill with a wonderful view of the surrounding hills with black faced sheep, grazing with bowed heads on the lower slopes. In the Borders, as in the Hebrides, the dead are provided with the best views, should they ever awaken to see them. We searched among the many headstones, wetting our feet in the long grass which the wind bent back. Finally, we came across the headstone which had been positioned in the older part of the cemetery. I felt a slight shock at seeing the name, James Knox carved on the lichened stone, as if I was looking at my own grave. An image came into my mind of that old man with his beard, his flat cap and his pipe, moving towards me on that last walk. We both kept walking and walking towards each other but the distance between us remained the same.

CHAPTER 13

Wood Smoke and Gorse

On our way back to Islay – my homecoming – the crossing from Gourock to East Loch Tarbert went smoothly, despite all our trepidations. On this occasion, my mother's belief in the benefits of sitting on the pages of a newspaper was well founded and she, as far as I can recall, avoided seasickness. However, in Tarbert, my mother had to endure further trauma. For reasons I can't recall, my father had some business to attend to in the small town and told us that he would get a taxi later in which he would bring our suitcases which never really recovered from their drenching in salt water. This was no great loss since they were very rarely used during the next six years we were to live on Islay. As there was no bus to take us to the ferry – the bus service was not designed solely for the convenience of passengers on the Islay ferry – my mother, George and myself set out to walk the mile and a half to the pier at West Loch Tarbert in the early autumn sunlight which made the wavelets in the harbour glisten, with a gentle breeze sounding through the rigging of the moored yachts. We left the town centre, passing the grey stone church which sat imperiously on a high mound looking down disdainfully on all who passed it by. It was when we took the narrow side road lined with trees which led to the pier at which the Islay ferry docked, that my mother noticed that in a clearing at the side of the road was an encampment of tinkers.

Among my mother's long list of fears was a fear of tinkers. Perhaps she had been told as a child those tales of gypsies stealing children and those tales had remained with her. Fear and prejudice tend to be handed down through the generations and I also felt a shiver of fear of those people whose lives seemed so unlike our own. I also felt a sense of guilt as I had recently stoned a tinker's tent. In the fifties and sixties, there were many travelling people on the Kintyre peninsula who were given the rather derogatory name of tinkers. The largest clan was the extended MacPhee family and some members of this family would come to Islay each year to perform back-breaking work on the island farms in the spring and summer. One of their regular encampments was in a hollow at the road end to Caol Ila and I would pass by their bender tents and see their washing laid over the gorse bushes which crackled on warm, sunlit days. One day on my way home from school, I and some of the pupils from Caol Ila, on seeing that the encampment was empty, stood on the mound above and rolled large stones and small boulders down to the tents in order to flatten them. Although the tents looked uninhabited, we had no way of knowing if a baby or an infant was inside one of them but that did not stop us. Nearly all of the adults we knew, including our parents, regarded tinkers as less than human and worthy of our contempt. Those attitudes influenced our behaviour towards people who lived differently to ourselves. The next afternoon as we passed the encampment, accompanied by the wife of the assistant distillery manager, a man came out of one of the bender tents and asked us if it was us who had stoned their tents yesterday. Of course, we denied all knowledge of the incident and the lady said that the innocent children in her charge would never do such a thing. I was struck by the gentleness and reasonableness of his voice. I began to realize that those travellers were no less human than I was. Part of me envied their apparent freedom to move from place to place but I saw that they were imprisoned by prejudice wherever they went.

There was another tinker family who came to Islay each summer and the father earned money not by working in the fields but by going around houses playing tunes on his bagpipes. I remember once he came up the drive to our house at Dunlossit and he stood with the wind ruffling his kilt which I expect was of MacPhee tartan. The tinker's wife stood some fifty yards behind and when he had stopped playing she shyly and cautiously approached our door and held out her husband's Glengarry in the hope that my mother would drop a penny or two into it. Despite her reservations about such people, I think that my mother would have enjoyed the diversion and the good old Scottish tunes such as the *Muckin' o' Geordie's Byre*, *Mairi's Wedding* and *Leaving Port Askaig* which she so longed to do.

But her pleasure at the pipe playing had now been forgotten when confronted by a whole tribe and my mother stood undecided whether she should continue or whether it would be safer to await her husband. Punctuality was never one of my father's strong points and my mother feared that he would arrive too late to catch the one ferry of the day, and we would be left standing at the roadside for hours on end. Having nowhere to spend the night compelled her to continue to the pier, holding the hands of her children. As we came closer, I saw the green canvas thrown over arched poles to make tents. I saw also the wood smoke from the fire encircled by stones rising lazily into the trees. I heard dogs barking in warning as we cautiously approached. We walked past the small group of men, women, and children with dark faces. I did my best to follow my mother's example and look the other way but part of me was curious to observe those people who I feared but at the same time felt strangely drawn to. One of the men called out a few words in greeting to my mother but it was difficult to make out what he said, either because of the thickness of his Highland accent or because he spoke in Gaelic, a language my mother detested. Either way, my mother looked the other way and did not respond and dragged my brother and me along with her.

Eventually, we reached the pier and waited anxiously for my father to arrive before the ferry sailed. It was with relief that we saw him get out of a car and remove our suitcases from the boot. We made our way up the gangway and found seats in the lower deck. My mother's sheets of newspaper worked their magic again and she reached Port Askaig without retching. We trooped down the gangway and on to the solid, familiar pier, exhausted after our *holiday* and I, for one, had no desire for another.

CHAPTER 14

Halfway to Paradise

In the days before television and record players, music was not often heard in many houses on Islay. There was a sort of silent lull for a few decades when islanders no longer met in each other's houses for ceilidhs, although there were ceilidhs held from time to time in the village halls on Islay. We did have a large *Murphy's* radio but my mother was never able to work it as she had a fear of any sort of powered gadget. The radio reception was poor and prone to interference. In summer when you turned on the radio using various knobs, there was no telling which station or which language you would hear. When my father did listen to the radio in the evening, it would mostly be news programmes but, at weekends, he would listen to comedies such as *Round the Horn*, *The Clitheroe Kid* – my favourite – and the one radio programme my mother liked: a family farce called *The McFlannels* which she looked forward to hearing each week. My father also liked detective series such as *Paul Temple*. It was rare to hear music coming from the radio so my mother would have welcomed hearing the bagpipe tunes.

On Sunday evenings, I would hear Radio Luxemburg coming from the transistor through the wall of my sisters' bedroom. Isabel, Catherine and Muriel shared the one small bedroom and from their window, you could glimpse the Sound of Islay through the spaces between the tapestry of branches and, across the sea, the bare hills of Jura. Radio Luxemburg was our only access to the latest pop hits. I would lie in bed and catch the voices, between the periods of interference and the Babel of foreign voices, of Jim Reeves, Skeeter Davis, Helen Shapiro, Adam Faith, Petula Clarke and, later, the Beatles and the Rolling Stones. There was a song called *James hold the*

Ladder Steady, which was often played around that time and which George used to mock me with as if the words were about me and the soppiness of romance. I was particularly moved by Petula Clarke, or it may have been Ann Shelton, singing *Sailor* with its lines:

> *Sailor, stop your roaming*
> *Sailor, leave the sea*
> *Sailor, when the tide turns*
> *Come home safe to me*

I could easily relate to those lines as the sea was such a constant presence in my life: its colours, its movement, its moods, its sounds and the sense of leaving, with the white hankies waved on the pier by those left behind like the beating of a seagull's wings. My response to a later line in the song: *To the harbour of my heart* was like my response to hearing my first lines of poetry by Walter de la Mare in the Big Room. I liked the sound of distant voices coming through the darkness as there was a sense of comfort in them. As a child, I often suffered from nightmares and a recurrent nightmare was that I had suddenly gone blind and I would awake to find myself grasping at the unseen walls, struggling to get out. When I wanted to avenge some sort of injustice or defeat which I had experienced, I would, in my imagination, bring out men from behind the walls who would act as my avenging angels. In my childish mind, the walls of that house in Dunlossit concealed so much. I think also that listening to the Sunday night pop music on that transistor radio was one of the few things in life which brought all three sisters together as I sensed a hostility between Isabel and Catherine who seemed to join forces against Muriel which was understandable, given Muriel's often unreasonable behaviour. A family, a large one, is a battleground from which no one leaves unscarred.

A still more exciting occurrence than listening to the latest hits on Radio Luxemburg through the box room walls on a Sunday evening was the day we got our first record player. It was a pebbled grey box with the name *Dansette* printed on it and you opened it up like a suitcase. Inside the case, was a turntable and a mechanical arm which placed singles or LPs on top of one another like a miniature version of the Jukebox I saw in the cafe in Bowmore. Now that we had a record player, all we needed was a record to play on it. We had to wait until my mother's next visit to Bowmore and hope that the only shop which sold records had a top twenty hit in its very limited stock. My mother returned with the only current hit the shop keeper could lay his hands on: *Halfway to Paradise* by Billy Fury. I watched with fascination the mechanical arm lift the single record on to the turntable and the needle gently lay itself on the revolving disc and, after a pregnant pause, there was the voice of Billy Fury sounding more loudly and more clearly than it ever did on Radio Luxembourg with its whistles and wheezes like my mother's bronchitis on a damp day in winter:

> *Put your sweet lips close to my lips*
> *And tell me that's where they're gonna stay*
> *Don't lead me halfway to paradise*
> *So near, yet so far away*
> *Oh, oh, oh, so near, yet so far*
> *So near, yet so far away*

Even at that early age, I could relate to those words, not in the sense of having experienced anything related to romantic love but the sense of yearning for something beyond my reach, of being aware of an underlying sense of dissatisfaction with life despite living in a place of such loveliness. That sense of longing for something other and indefinable has remained with me and I gained some comfort from those words, however seemingly trite, knowing that others have experienced this sense of longing for something more: *so near, yet so far away.* Whenever I hear this song, that late afternoon in Dunlossit with myself and my family standing around a box – we were too excited to sit – listening intently to a human voice arising mysteriously comes back to me so vividly. Noel Coward was quite correct, there are few things in life which possess the potent power of what he perhaps unfairly called *cheap music.*

On Saturday afternoons, my sisters would iron out the creases from their best dresses to the background of music in the excited preparation of going to a dance in Bowmore. A white sheet was laid on the kitchen table in order to make up for the absence of an ironing board and the heavy iron would be placed on top of the range to heat. Through the kitchen window in summer, raindrops would gather on the red stamens of the fuchsia bush and our cat would lie stretched out on the lumpy settee, with the coal shifting in the grate as flames consumed them. In the spaces between the recorded sounds, I would hear the faint notes of the sea as it made its own music.

My mother retained her fondness for a few of the songs of Robert Burns which she learnt at school. Her favourite was one of the loveliest of all the songs attributed to Burns, *Ca The Yowes* with its sweet ache of longing for the time when all fears will be comforted through love and which must have brought back something of her childhood memories of the Borders landscape with its steep, sheep strewn hillsides:

> *We'll gae down by Cluden side,*
> *Thro' the hazels spreading wide,*
> *O'er the waves that sweetly glide*
> *To the moon sae clearly.*

The waves referred to in this song are not the waves of the Atlantic which she so much feared but the gentler waves of the River Nith which flows into the Solway Firth.

My father's taste in music was rather more limited than my mother's but in brief moments of happiness or reverie, he would sing snatches of *I'll Take You Home Again Kathleen* which he must have remembered from his childhood. Perhaps the song reminded him of his mother who was called Catherine who, unlike my mother's father, came once to stay with us on Islay, along with Uncle Jack and his fiancé, Mary. My granny spent the entire time with us – it seemed so much longer than a week – plotting to separate Jack and Mary, without much success. She died a few years after her one and only visit, in her nineties, worn out with hard work and cantankerousness.

On Saturday evenings my father would sometimes return late from the pub at Port Askaig, where the barmaid would sing snatches from Andy Stewart's *Campbeltown Loch, I wish you were whisky*. Only occasionally would my mother go with her husband, partly because she was never much of a one for alcohol, and she would sit ill at ease in the snug, her beady eye on the carryings-on of others who should know better, genteelly sipping a *Babycham* or a *Snowball* with an exotic cherry floating on top. Each Hogmanay, she would take a small glass of *Harvey's Bristol Cream* to see out the old and bring in the new as she listened to Kenneth McKellar sing *The Rowan Tree* for the umpteenth time on the television Hogmanay Party which had been recorded in October.

Sometimes after his night in the pub, my father would somehow make his way up the dark drive on unsteady feet and as soon as he entered the kitchen, he would put a record on the turntable and turn the volume up as far as it would go as if only loud music could penetrate his befuddled brain. The record he chose to play at full blast would invariably be the *Waters of Kyleskue:*

> *There's many a mile from Melness to the Waters of Kyleskue*
> *O'er all of Bonnie Scotland I dearly love the west,*
> *It's bens and glens in summer time, they surely are the best;*
> *There's grandeur and there's beauty in those Hills when passing through*

Mercifully, after a few deafening repeats of this song and his increasingly discordant attempts to sing along, all that could be heard from my father's hard chair – he felt more comfortable sitting on hard surfaces – were loud snores.

CHAPTER 15

The World Viewed Through Snow

Surprisingly, my father was one of the first people at our end of the island to get a television set – a second hand one, of course. By our end of the island, I mean the parish of Kilmeny in the north-east of Islay. At that time, the Church of Scotland was still an important influence and islanders still identified strongly with their parish.

My father was a lifelong Rangers supporter and as a child and a youth, he would attend the occasional match at Ibrox Park when he had saved up sufficient money. When he was small, he would ask an adult to lift him over the turnstile so that he could get in for free. In 1961, Rangers reached the first ever European Cup Winner's Final and the second leg – it was played over two legs – was held at Ibrox Park and was to be shown live on television. This must have compelled my father to get his hands on this new-fangled device.

Just as my father spent hours tinkering with the wick of the paraffin lamp, never satisfied with the flame and just as he kept turning the knobs of the wireless to get a clearer sound, he would spend even more hours trying to get a picture from this television box. As he could not find anyone on the island to fix a television aerial on the chimney, the ariel was perched in the attic in a desperate attempt to get a signal. He would trudge up and down the stairs and the step ladder to adjust the angle of the aerial and finding that it made little difference, he would twiddle with the knobs of the television yet again. There would be a slightly clearer picture during the winter months but in summer, all you could see was ghost-like figures moving through a blizzard of interference. The Rangers final which my father was so anxious to witness unfortunately took place in summer when the television reception was at its worst. The match appeared to take place during a snowstorm with the football resembling a snowball. In all too brief moments, you could see the blurred outline of moving players chasing after something. As Rangers lost, the inability to see the match may have offered some small consolation.

Despite the frustrations involved in trying to watch the small, convex screen through a blizzard, I gained a good deal of pleasure from watching certain programmes, particularly in winter when, ironically, the snow ceased falling on the screen. I would look forward to coming home from school when I was still in the Wee Room to watch *Bill and Ben* – the flower-pot men with *Little Weed* who sounded a bit like the headmaster at Keills school whose voice rose several octaves when he lost his temper. *Squeak* was in charge of the Big Room and I wasn't looking forward to that monumental step next door which was the punishment which awaited you for growing older. Another programme I liked was the *Woodentops*, I was never keen on the soppy *Andy Pandy*. One advantage of watching those puppet programmes with such a poor reception was that I could not detect the strings which made those figures more real.

Later, my brother and I came to look forward to our weekly indulgence in *The Lone Ranger* and my favourite, *The Range Rider* with his assistant, Dick West, the *all-American boy* – whatever that meant. Those tall, slim men with their tight black jeans and with their six shooters encased in their holsters had a big influence in my imaginative life. When I went up the drive to the walled garden, I would not walk but trot, slapping my sides as if I was on a sleek stallion. My favourite toy was a silver-coloured revolver which fired caps which left the smell of what to me was gunpowder after each bang. Like much else on Islay, those magical caps could only be bought in one shop in Bowmore and I would ask my mother to get me more caps when she next visited the 'metropolis'.

Television, what we could see of it, opened a world of seeming glamour to islanders who for much of each year inhabited a world of mud, drizzle, drudgery and midges. The man who assisted my father in the garden and grounds, Dan Macaulay lived alone, exiled from Campbeltown. He was astonished the first time he saw *Top of the Pops* on our television set, by what a vibrant world the pop stars and dancers appeared to live in. Through those black and white images, mostly white, he imagined a world of colour and excitement, a life so remote from his own. I think that the coming of television to remote places such as the Hebrides bred a sense of dissatisfaction, a sense that real life lay elsewhere, which increased the sense of longing among young people, to leave as soon as they could. The *mainland* took on the status of a mythical land, a vague place in which dreams could be realised. It is true that throughout history and especially since the Clearances which affected Islay in the late 18th and early 19th centuries as in so many other parts of the Highlands and Islands, emigration was an inescapable aspect of life, but it was then driven largely by force of economic necessity. But now there were subtler, more intangible forces which influenced people to leave the place of their birth.

Despite my mother's dislike of Gaelic, she came to look forward to the one regular weekly Gaelic television programme, '*Se Ur Beatha* with its mostly cheerful, foot tapping songs. I doubt if my mother ever knew, or bothered to find out, that the title of the programme meant *You're Welcome*, ironically, as she never really felt welcome on Islay. The presenter of the programme, the singer, Calum Kennedy became a favourite with my mother and my sisters and his LPs added to our very limited stock of records.

Perhaps not surprisingly given that my father's hobby was also his job, the only programme he really looked forward to, apart from the brief highlights of Scottish football on a Saturday evening, was *Gardeners' World* presented by Percy Thrower. I found myself looking out for the moment in the programme when Percy would step into his greenhouse, take off his jacket and hang it on a nail.

I should state that we never paid for a television licence on Islay and my father felt justified in doing so as we could only get a more-or-less clear image on the screen during winter months. Before going to bed, my mother would always place a small tablecloth over the television and this remained on the set until it was switched on the next day. One afternoon, out of the blue, a van which checked if you possessed a television licence came up the

Dunlossit drive and stopped below our house. Not seeing an aerial fixed around our chimney pot, a man came to our door and my mother invited him in. On seeing a box covered with a cloth, he naturally assumed that it was a cage for a budgie and left. It's just as well that he didn't wait for the budgie to sing.

CHAPTER 16

Watching from Afar

Between rhododendron bushes, I would create a hollow which I regarded as my hideout, rather like the bank robbers in a cowboy film. I would sit in my place of refuge and look out in secret on the world around me. I liked to sit in my hollow especially on a windy day, when I could hear the waves crashing against the rocks below our house, there were many such days on Islay, and feel safe and sheltered. I liked it when someone passed, and I could observe them without being seen. I remember one day when I was hiding in the hollow near the side of the drive, I watched my mother pass with her usual blue coat and carrying her large shopping bag on her way to catch the bus to Bowmore and I did not let on I was there. One afternoon, I hid in my rhododendron hollow when the assistant manager of Caol Ila distillery, a Mr Manley who had two equally obnoxious daughters and who spoke in a posh English accent, drove up to our house to take me to his elder daughter's birthday party. I heard my mother calling out my name repeatedly but I stayed hidden and silent. I knew that he would be coming to collect me and I simply did not want to go, as I felt that I would feel out of place among the other children and I did not like the two Manley girls who I felt regarded themselves as being somehow superior to me with their middle class voices and ways. Living on a private estate made me aware from an early age of class distinctions. When the Big House was occupied in the long summer months, I would often see the children of the Schroders and their wealthy guests out playing, but it never occurred to me or my brother to join them in their games. It is not even that my parents forbade us to do so, it was just an unspoken assumption that there was a gulf between us which could not be bridged.

One evening, my family was invited to a musical event which was held in the Big House. However, when we arrived, we were informed that we were to sit on the staircase which led down to the drawing room in which stood the singers and musicians surrounded by our social superiors who sat on plush sofas, leather armchairs and elegant upholstered chairs. My family, along with a few other workers on the estate, were left to sit with their knees level with their chins on the hard stairs and look down enviously on those privileged guests below. That evening brought home to me, more than anything else had done before, the unbridgeable gulf between those who resided in the Big House and those of us who didn't.

One of my most recurring memories of my childhood is of looking down on a world of which I was not a part. Often, I would join my father and brother, and sometimes my mother, in late afternoons standing beside a tree on the drive looking down on the pier at Port Askaig when the ferry arrived from the mainland. As the ship neared the pier, it would sidle in and ropes were thrown to the pier man like cowboys throwing lassoes around bucking steers. We would enjoy the bustle and the busyness for an hour or so as people made their way, burdened by suitcases, down the gangway. The steepness of the gangway would depend on how high the tide was. I liked it when the incline was steep and the passengers' descent to the pier was precarious. Even from a distance, I could see the ropes which attached the boat to the pier straining and knew that if I was standing closer, I would hear them groan. When the passengers had disembarked, cars and other vehicles would be raised from the bowels of the ferry on a winch with thick netting around them. The car as it was lifted would veer out to sea in a strong gust of wind and it looked as though it would be drowned until at the last moment, it was drawn in to land, more-or-less undamaged, on the pier.

There were the red *MacBraynes* buses parked on the pier. One bus would go to Port Ellen and the other to Portnahaven where the seals congregated in the horseshoe bay. In the spring and summer months, some passengers would make their way along the pier to the whitewashed walls of Port Askaig hotel. Others made their way to the shop just across the road from the hotel. I would hear the raised voices and the laughter sound from the echo chamber of the pier to reach us where we stood gazing down. When all the passengers had made their way from the ferry, another group of people would begin to board, making their unsteady way up the gangway with dreams of what they might find on the mainland where life was perceived to move differently. Some boarding the ferry would be setting off on holiday, usually to stay with relatives, as we did. The better off would look forward to a week or two in a hotel or guest house, more likely in Scotland but sometimes beyond. Some passengers would be returning to their mainland lives after a brief return to the island of their birth, perhaps now wondering why they ever left in the first place. There would be a few islanders who had decided that they would leave Islay behind, perhaps never to return, not knowing that the island would one day, sooner or later, draw them back. Some of those boarding would be making their way to hospital in Glasgow for tests, fearful of what the result might be. There might perhaps be someone also who would be making his or her way to the psychiatric hospital in Lochgilphead which was something of a shameful secret which was kept within families. That hospital was a background threat in the lives of some islanders. If their depression or delusions got out of control, they would be sent to that place, never knowing when they would be allowed to return home. All those who ascended that gangway carried not only their suitcases but their dreams or fears. I read somewhere that the trouble with leaving is that you have to take yourself with you.

Occasionally, a hearse would be waiting on the pier and men in black suits would walk up the gangway, go on board and come down later carrying a coffin shoulder high, stepping slowly and cautiously. The deceased may well have been someone who left the island when they were in their teens or twenties in search of work or in search of the fulfilment of what life might offer if only they could get away. However, the longing to return remains: some are fortunate to return when they are alive but for others, it is only death which brings them home so that they can lie beneath the loved turf they stepped on as a child, amid the headstones engraved with remembered names. I'd watch the hearse make its stately way up the steep, winding brae between the ash trees and around the sharp corner from where those, still with eyes to see, can look down the entire length of the Sound of Islay on days when the mist has lifted with the pencilled outline of Colonsay in the distance. The hearse would follow the narrow road to one of the island cemeteries: Kilmeny with its broken chapel, cradled in the cup of gently sloping fields where cattle graze on the lush grass of summer. Or perhaps, the hearse would move on to the graveyard behind the Round Church which looks down on Bowmore and across Loch Indaal with its ever-altering lights or to Portnahaven or the graveyard at Kilnaughton within sound of the waves folding over themselves on the sanded shore, shadowed by the soaring wings of sea eagles in search of prey.

Whenever I now return to Islay many, many, years later, I follow the track through the woodland with its fallen rainbow of wild flowers in spring and summer and where winds rustle the sunset coloured leaves of autumn, from Kilmeny Church to the graveyard and browse around the headstones. To read the names and dates on the headstones is like reading a fragmented memoir of my childhood. Here is the grave of the lady, Mrs Pate, whose house in Caol Ila I attended Sunday school year after year, singing hymns such as:

Jesus loves me! This I know,
For the Bible tells me so.

If I ever possessed such a simplistic faith, I have long since lost it. I find myself wondering if she encountered at her death the gentle face of Christ which was depicted in the illustrated Bible which she read to the children who sat in a circle around her in that small living-room with the patter of a passing shower on the windowpanes. She lies now with her husband, George who led the Life Boys in which myself and others would march round and round the school hall at Keills Primary each Wednesday evening with the coarse navy blue shorts itching my sweating legs.

On another row of headstones is the grave of the man nicknamed Calum Pin as he was so tall and thin and who often staggered out of Port Askaig pub on Saturday evenings to make his way to the outside toilet, passing George and me as we sat on the whitewashed wall outside waiting on our father to bring us out a textured bottle of *Pepsi* and a packet of Oxo flavoured crisps. Once when Calum was even more drunk than usual, he handed us a five-pound note which seemed a fortune to us as it was some two hundred times greater than our weekly pocket money. We came to regret telling our father of this unexpected windfall as he made us return it. I had dreams of spending the fortune on tubes of *Spangles* or *Refreshers*, *Duncan's* whole nut chocolate, *Fry's Five Centres*, *Lucky Bags* – despite their disappointing contents – a family block of *Walls* ice-cream all to myself or half a dozen *Lyons Maid Mivis:* the possibilities seemed endless. However, like so many of my dreams, they came to nothing.

There is the grave of Donald, the man who drove the *MacBraynes* bus from Port Askaig to Port Ellen for decade after decade and who gave George and me a lift to school each Tuesday and Thursday as those were the mornings when the *Lochiel* would come into Port Askaig. My father would help him in his garden in Keills, in his rare moments of spare time to return the favour of those free lifts. There was the grave of the woman who once lived in a cottage thatched with heather and who was once found attempting to cut her lawn with a pair of scissors. I read the engraved words on the headstone of the man who caught the ropes on the pier, thrown from the ferry. There are the graves of two of my fellow pupils at Keills school, taken too early due to their abuse of alcohol, seeking their dreams not on some mythical mainland but in a bottle. I come across the grave of the only disabled person I knew on the island who drove a tiny car in the shape of a bubble and whose transparent roof would lift up like a skylight. There are the graves of those who worked on Dunlossit Estate when I was a child: gamekeepers, tenant farmers, forestry workers and those whose lungs were choked by dust after many years working in the limestone quarry only a mile or so from where they lie now with the island they knew and loved spread out above them, deaf to the haunting cries of the curlew.

There is more recently, the grave of my brother-in-law, Donald Morrison, the man Catherine married after she had dumped her cat throwing boyfriend. Donald would take George and myself out some Sundays in his green *Mini* van and we would often stop at Bruichladdich shop as it was the first ever on

Islay to open its doors on a Sunday. Somehow, ice-cream and sweets tasted more of a treat when bought on the Sabbath. On some sun caressed days in summer, Donald would take us to the beach at Kilchoman where I would feel the shell sand between my bare toes and watch the Atlantic breakers rush in. The ink on the card which Catherine placed on her husband's grave with the words: *Sleep tight, my darling* was soon dissolved by rain but the love remains somewhere deep beneath in a secret place where her dementia cannot reach.

I stand on the mound beside the broken walls of the ancient chapel, the wind combing the long grass with the fields and low hills of Islay spread out before me, touched from time to time by fugitive slivers of sunlight beneath a fathomless sky. This graveyard is a meeting place for those who remained on the island and those who left but returned home. The rows of headstones are like the joining of hands in those playground games when we ran round and round in circles with no beginning and no end in sight.

CHAPTER 17

Pan Drops and Sermons

Kilmeny Church played an important role in our lives and it provided one of the few social events in my mother's life. On most Sunday mornings, she would walk down the drive in her best blue coat – she had two navy blue coats, one for outings and one for everyday wear. There would be a navy blue hat perched upon her head which she only wore for church and which she struggled to keep on in gusts of wind. There was her small Bible, which she hardly ever opened, in her gloved hand and her precious handbag slung over her wrist, with her face pallored by powder. The face powder, contained in a round, silver coated compact with a mirror inside its top lid, was my mother's only concession to makeup. Also, inside her bag, was a coin for the collection plate and a poke of Pan Drops to see her through the sermon which she only intermittently listened to but she enjoyed the hymns she sang as a child such as *All People that on Earth do Dwell* and *The Old Rugged* Cross. The organist at Kilmeny, Katy McGee, was rather hard of hearing and she tended to play so loudly that she drowned out the singing of the congregation. Given some of the voices in the church, this might be seen as something of a blessing. Katy was not only a musician but also a writer of verses to mark special occasions in the parish such as the fleeting visit of a member of the Royal family to the Lifeboat station in Port Askaig, sponsored by Mr Schroder, or a birth or death. As it often rained and was too windy for an umbrella to stay up, my mother's bag also contained that trusted friend, her rain mate: a see-through polythene hat with a cord to tie under the chin which lacked a certain elegance. Going to church, along with her shopping trips to Bowmore and the very occasional whist drive was one of those few regular social activities in her life in which she could meet people from outside her family. There was also the added bonus of a *hurl* on the four-mile bus journey to the church and back again, and the chance of a blether after the service.

In the 1950s and 60s, the church played a fairly central role in the parish although there were already signs of a decline in church going. Nonetheless, almost everyone came to be christened, married and to attend the final service which they would not hear.

I have a blurred photo of myself as a baby in my mother's arms as she stood with my father and the young minister, the Revd Charlton outside Kilmeny Church on the day of my christening beneath the arch of trees. No doubt, the rooks would have been calling from the bare winter branches, a sound I always associate with that secluded church reached by a sloping, gravel drive. In his fervour and frustration at the lack of devotion among his parishioners, the Revd Charlton once led services up the brae in the middle of the small village of Ballygrant but, I gather, it was not an experiment which he often repeated. Religious fervour, if it ever existed on Islay, had long since evaporated among the population. There are, however, reminders throughout the island of those who came here to be closer to God in the distant past. There are the remains of small cells in which a solitary monk endured rain and storms, surviving on whatever scraps of food came his way, striving to move closer to a mysterious Being, searching for subtle signs of His fleeting presences; hearing echoes of His voice in the wind; glimpsing His shadow as it passed across grass; seeing Christ's ghost step along moonlit paths over the bay as if striding towards him: closer and closer only to dissolve as he reached out to touch Him. There were the standing stones on the hill reaching up as if in prayer and the stone crosses with their carvings of the unbroken circle of birth and death. There are the churches on remote parts of the island, now largely deserted of people, where all that remain are the gable ends and the tower with its bell which only the wind rings, calling and calling out for the congregation which has gone.

The Revd Charlton did not stay long as Islay was no place for his fervent, evangelistic sermons which were inclined to continue long after the first

Pan Drop had been sucked and the rummaging around in handbags for the second one tended to create too much rustling when the sermon was still going on. Then came a succession of ministers or what were called missionaries which was the name given to those who were not fully qualified as ministers. One such missionary who had several children, seemed to struggle to make ends meet and my father often gave him vegetables to take away on his frequent visits to the garden. Although my father would accompany his wife to church only when he could spare time from work in the garden, usually in the autumn and winter when there was less watering and tending of plants to do in the greenhouses, he saw rather a lot of this particular preacher without having to listen to his sermons.

As a member of the Sunday school and the Life Boys, attending Kilmeny Church on special occasions was a regular occurrence throughout my childhood. There was an excitement about attending the Watchnight service on Christmas Eve when I would sit up on the balcony – long since gone – and look down on the congregation below me. As the voices rose with the words of carols such as *Hark! The Herald Angels Sing* and *O Come All Ye Faithful*, their rousing refrains would send a shiver through me and the gentler carols such as *Child in A Manger* would instil that old sense of longing for something other. The archaic nature of the words appealed to me as it evoked that sense of mystery and grandeur which was far removed from the demotic, all-mates-together tone which so many churches have now adopted in the increasingly desperate attempt to fill pews. The very awkwardness of the language of the King James Bible to modern ears helps us to realise that we are striving to express what no human words can express.

On one stormy Christmas Eve, I attended the service without my parents and I got a lift back with James Carmichael, along with Duncan MacPhee, who lived in the Lodge at the head of Dunlossit drive. James helped out with the Life Boys and was one of the few parishioners who not only possessed a car, but an odd shaped, exotic sounding car at that: a Volkswagen Beetle. Instead of driving me up the few hundred yards to my house – perhaps he was in a hurry to see his lady friend – I was dropped off at the Lodge, along with Duncan, and expected to make my own way up the dark drive with no

CHAPTER 18

Seeing the World for the First Time

As a member of the Life Boys, I would visit most of the Church of
Scotland churches on Islay: the Round Church in Bowmore, St. John's
Church in Port Ellen and the churches in Port Charlotte and Portnahaven.
As the hymn, *Onward Christian Soldiers* indicates, there was believed to be
a curious connection between Christianity and marching. I rather enjoyed
the marching, however pointless it may have seemed. My most memorable
experience of attending a service in another church occurred one Sunday
evening in summer in the church of St. Kiaran's which is situated between
Bruichladdich and Port Charlotte. Every aspect of that evening service has
stayed with me throughout the years. It was one of those evenings in which
the island was dazzled by sunlight and I felt as if I had stepped inside a
diamond and looked out at the altered facets of the world where everything
appeared in a sharper and clearer focus. The church stands looking out across
Loch Indaal which almost divides the island into two. Coming from Port
Askaig, you turn right at the island crossroads of Bridgend and as you follow
the narrow road around the sea loch, you enter a different landscape in which
the lush fields slope gently down towards the sea. There is a spaciousness
and openness about the landscape along the Rhinns which you don't
find anywhere else on Islay and a different quality of light which is reflected
off the loch which holds a mirror to the sky with its ever-altering tapestry
of blue depths and cloud. Most of the fields were unfenced and sheep and
cattle would wander lazily across the road, only occasionally disturbed by
passing traffic. In spring, black faced lambs would call out when they were
lost and be found again by their mothers who stood patiently over them as

their young greedily fed. Across the road, oystercatchers wearing their white aprons stabbed their orange beaks into the pale sand between the rocks and pebbles, the sunlight revealing their blue veins. Across the loch, Bowmore with its whitewashed houses shimmered in the distance; the Round Church perched imperiously above the village. As I gazed out to where Loch Indaal met the open sea, the etched outline of the cliffs of the Mull of Oa could be seen.

As I sat in the back of the minibus. I could see the distillery at Bruichladdich and a couple of miles further on, we stopped at St. Kiaran's, the church named after the Celtic saint who was said to have transformed the water in a well so that it tasted like wine or honey. I remember following the leader of the Life Boys, George Pate, up the gravel path which led to the entrance of the dark stoned building with its small arched windows like eyelids and its varnished door open as if to let the sea light in. The rows of polished pews shone beneath the roof which arched like an ark. I followed the others down to the front of the church and I found myself sitting close to an old lady – she seemed old to my childish eyes – who played the organ. I cannot now recall what hymns she played but I recall how her fingers moved delicately across the keyboard, the keys seeming to slow waltz beneath her touch. I experienced an almost trance-like state just watching the pressed keys rise and fall and hear the differing tones they made. The sunlight which filtered through the narrow, lead-crossed windows seemed to caress both the organ and the lady who played it and dust motes danced across the pews on to the array of hats which nearly all the female members of the congregation wore. I felt a kind of peace, my usual feelings of anxiety dissolving momentarily as if I too had dipped my fingers deep into a well and brought out the taste of honey to my lips.

That feeling of peace which I had experienced inside the church was heightened still more when I filed out of the building and through the narrow door to be met with the dancing lights on the sea. It was as if I was seeing the world for the first time and everything seemed new, beautiful and strange. I heard the cries of the sea birds as they veered across the blue sky, their flight mirrored on the motionless surface of the loch. The winds, for once, held their breath, the distant bleating of the sheep and the lowing of the cattle blended their echoes in the stilled air.

That was an evening which has stayed with me throughout my life. It was an experience which has never been repeated and it has become a place of refuge which I hold in my mind.

James' paternal grandfather and family

Gardener's Cottage, Dunlossit

The Potting Shed, Dunlossit

Inside the walled garden at Dunlossit in the early 1960s

Granny Chisholm's house beyond the walled garden

Looking down to the 'Wee Pier', Dunlossit

*Back Lawn
at Dunlossit*

James' sister Catherine in the greenhouse

Waterfall at Dunlossit

*Children and schoolmistress (Mrs Fisher) of Keills School 'Wee Room'.
James is third from left in back row.*

*Children and schoolmaster ('Squeak') of Keills School 'Big Room'.
James is fourth from left in back row.*

Postcard view of Port Askaig

'Lochiel' at Port Askaig pier

Loch Indaal

Paps of Jura

Reflections on the Lily Loch

Loch Allan boatshed

Kilmeny Church

Ruins of church in Kilmeny cemetery

James' friend Donald James MacPhee in later years in the Deer Room at Dunlossit

Donald James MacPhee, who went on to become Head Gamekeeper, outside Dunlossit

MacArthur's Head lighthouse

CHAPTER 19

Walking on Water

It was rare for snow to lie on Islay given the influence of the Gulf Stream – according to *Squeak*, it was more correctly called the North Atlantic Drift – but there was one memorable morning when I was aged around nine or ten and I awoke to a land muffled by deep snow. Even before I drew back the curtains of the small box room window which I shared with my brother, I could sense the depth of silence as if all sounds had been hushed. A line of poetry I had recently learned at school came into my mind: *And no birds sang.*

I looked out from the window and saw the familiar scenes of Dunlossit transformed. The trees held armfuls of snow in their branches. The sandstone walls of the yard were draped with white and the window slats of the larder in which the dead birds hung were layered with ice. The espaliered apple trees on the wall merged with the whitewash of the wall and the sloping roof of the coalhouse was like something out of a Christmas card. On the path from our house, I saw patterns of footprints, no doubt made by my father as he made his way to the garden to check that the greenhouses had maintained some warmth from the paraffin heaters which would glow more brightly with the glass made opaque by snow.

As I sat at the kitchen table, gazing through the sugar frosted branches of sycamores to catch glimpses of the metallic grey of the sea, my father came in with the checked flat cap pressed half-way down his reddened ears, flapping his arms in and out like an animated scarecrow to generate some semblance of warmth. As always on wintry days, he said: *You're lucky you're in the hoose.* He also added the far less accustomed words: *There'll be no school for you the day.*

George who tended to get up before me was also given this unexpected holiday. We went into the yard and saw that the cobbles had been smoothed over by the snow. We kicked the ball to each other but quickly got bored as the ball kept getting stuck as it increased in size like a rolled snowball. We went into the garage in which the motor mowers were kept. There was another door which led from the garage into a room which held a piano whose damp keys I would thump with my fists or climb up and walk across the keys to create a tuneless din. I must have spent many hours hammering away at that piano during the wet days of summer or the finger numbing days of winter without creating a single tune.

Bored with my piano 'playing', I then threw punches at the *Freddy Mills* punch ball which was my most wanted Christmas gift. Boxing had become the latest craze among the boys at Keills and it was this that made me long for a punch ball and boxing gloves so that I could practise and be ready for my next big fight. But after a while, I found that I grazed my knuckles through the flimsy gloves as I hit the coarse ball so I gave that up after a short time. I found, as I so often did, that a holiday from school delivers less than it promises. So much of the pleasure in holidays lies in their anticipation, rather like one's dreams of what one might do when grown-up.

My favourite activity on rare days of severe frost was to go ice skating on the shallow loch which lay in a cupped hollow between low hills past Loch Allan. George and I would pester our father to take an hour or so away from his precious greenhouses and potting sheds to walk the mile or so to test the thickness of the ice on the loch by throwing whatever boulders he could find on the shore to see if the ice withstood the impacts. We'd wait with bated breath to hear the report on his return as to whether or not the loch was safe to skate on. If the report was favourable, we would go down to the Gate Lodge and ask if our playmates, Duncan and Donald James, wanted to come with us. If they did, the four of us would set off up the brae behind the yard and follow the limestoned drive past the horse chestnut trees where we gathered their fallen treasure in autumn and stamped on their spiky cases to reveal the shiny mahogany nuts which lay within. We'd go down the brae which leads to the Lily Loch whose surface was made motionless by a film of ice which faintly mirrored the sky. We never skated on the Lily Loch as it was too deep and it did not freeze sufficiently beneath its canopy of trees. We'd continue past the turn off to Loch Allan with its boat house thatched with heather and from where we would take the rowing boat out on the loch to trawl for brown trout without the gamekeeper's permission.

We crossed the small bridge across the burn and up past the gate which leads to Kilslevan, where my father once discovered a nest of pheasant eggs which he collected in his flat cap, and followed a path through thick woodland stepping across tussocky, frosted grass which crackled beneath our feet until we reached the lochan whose ice glistened in fleeting glimpses of sunlight.

We could not afford ice skates; our skates were our wellies and we would do our best to run across the ice to gather enough speed to slide for a few yards with our arms spread wide to help our balance. I experienced a sense of freedom in those brief glides across the surface with the knowledge that beneath the ice lay a few feet of water and I liked that sensation of walking on water. When not attempting to skate, we'd throw boulders on the loch and listen to the ice shudder as the boulders landed with the sound of its impact spread out across the surface like the echoes of waves from a sea cave. Sometimes, a crack would appear on the ice and I'd feel a shiver of fear as I felt the surface vibrate beneath my feet. We'd sometimes slide the boulders across the ice like curling stones – we had seen curling played on television. As so much of what we watched on television took part in a blizzard, curling seemed an appropriate sport for the conditions.

As dusk began its slow descent over the hills and fields, we would make our way back through the darkening wood, disturbing a pheasant or two who appeared without warning from the dead bracken, quickening our heart beats. Above the Lily Loch, sometimes there was a stag standing stock still, scenting the air for danger like a connoisseur nosing a single malt in a tulip-shaped glass. Across the surface of the loch, shadows shivered, forming pathways through the rigid reeds. We knew that the ice could not last for long, perhaps tomorrow it would be gone and it could be years before it would return and the knowledge of its rarity and brevity heightened the pleasure of those few hours in which we could glide across water without wetting our feet.

CHAPTER 20

Circles of Time

Although *Squeak* was a moody and bad-tempered man and, in many respects, not suited to dealing with children, I gained quite a lot during the four years I spent in the Big Room at Keills. At first sight, his black beard with grey tinges gave him a rather fierce appearance. After his wife left him, I sensed that he struggled on the domestic front. He wore a shiny, white plastic collar but beneath the collar, his white shirt had a yellowish tinge. He would not have been offered a role in a *Persil* advert. As well as a demanding job as headmaster in the two-teacher school, he had been left with three children: two boys and a girl and he was involved in the Church of Scotland as a missionary of sorts. He and his children lived in the small cottage a few yards from the school. I sensed that his eldest son who was not at all academically minded but vain and spent much time each day slicking backward and forward his hair, greased with *Brylcreem*, in order to form a quiff, in a fanciful attempt to look like Elvis Presley, caused him particular concern and was one of the causes of his frequent bad moods.

Of course, catering for four classes in the one classroom must have been a demanding task, given that the children under his charge were of a wide range of abilities. One of his pupils had learning difficulties and he remained at Keills long after the age at which he would normally have gone on to the secondary school at Bowmore. The boy's name was Sandy and he sat at a desk at the back of the room. Unable to teach him much, *Squeak* spent years trying to teach Sandy to tell the time and would have him draw clock face after clock face in his dog-eared jotter. Sandy would form the circles of the clock face by drawing his often blunt pencil, around an old penny and then draw imaginary clock hands with the aid of his chewed ruler. Although Sandy often looked rather bored and bewildered by this seemingly never-ending task, he would sometimes look quite absorbed as he followed his own motions of time with his tongue protruding through his decayed teeth. I once looked through his jotter and as I turned the smudged pages, my eyes were met with page after page of clock faces. It wasn't always easy to tell the times as Sandy would often forget to make one hand longer than the other. He appeared to live in times of his own making. Given that there seemed no progression in his life as he sat at the same desk year after year, for Sandy, time had stopped. It was as if he lived in an eternal present with no past and no future.

He was much taller and stronger than all the other pupils and he would give the other children rides on his back as if he was a horse. When he was not doing that, he would stand in a corner of the playground and watch the other boys play football. One day we played football on the muddy field when we were warned not to and we were late coming in after the bell sounded. *Squeak*, who was in one of his bad moods that day, belted all the boys, including Sandy who was only standing watching. All of us felt that burning sense of injustice.

By the age of fourteen, Sandy's face was marked by signs of age, it was if, despite the slow motions of his clock faces, time had moved more quickly for him without his knowing. He lived with his mother, a tall woman who had the nickname of *Snowdrop* because of the tendency of her head to droop, on a small croft a mile or so out of Keills and Sandy would work on the croft, on which there were no set times to adhere to. I heard later that time ran out for him when he was still, chronologically, a young man. In his life, as in his schooling, the motions of his clock hands ceased.

Squeak was at his most effective as a teacher not when he bored us all with arithmetic, algebra, the history of kings and queens, English grammar and so on but when he got sidetracked and talked of his passion for those people of the distant past who had inhabited Islay. He wrote a booklet of Gaelic place names and the meanings behind them. Although I have forgotten the details, he did instil in me a sense of the long habitation of the island and the mysterious nature of the culture and beliefs. Only fragments of their lives remain: the broken chapels in remote parts of the island; the outlines of beehive cells; the brochs; the standing stones; the crannogs; the Celtic Cross at Kildalton; the remains of the home of the Lords of the Isles at Finlaggan. On one or two occasions, when he must have been in a particularly good mood, *Squeak* took us up to the ancient graveyard a few hundred yards above the school, each of us holding a sheet of paper and a pencil, and demonstrated to his pupils the art of stone rubbing. As I held my paper against an ornately carved headstone, made more intricate with lichens, in the shelter provided by the graveyard wall, I saw as I moved my pencil back and forth over the paper, the emergence of circles and crosses and symbols. It was as if my pencil was revealing patterns of the past. I sensed that I was part of an immeasurably long line of people who had lived on this island and, however accidental my family's coming to Islay was and however unwanted my birth might well have been, I somehow belonged here. Much more through accident than design, I had found a home.

As in the Wee Room, I gradually worked my way towards a desk at the wide window of the Big Room as the years progressed. At the start of each new school year, you moved to the next row of desks to your left. There were about sixteen pupils in the Big Room at that time, approximately four pupils to each class. We were given a lesson in Gaelic each week but the few in the school who were native speakers of Gaelic had an obvious advantage when it came to the annual test in the subject. *Squeak* had little patience for those non-Gaelic speakers such as myself and tended to make fun of my attempts at pronunciation. Similarly, he would set essay topics, in English, which I rather enjoyed and, occasionally, I felt that I had written a piece which I was rather proud of. When my essay was returned to me, I would see red ink marks all over it, pointing to my spelling and grammatical errors. I found this rather disheartening and I felt that it stunted whatever creative powers I possessed.

However, *Squeak* did instil the beginnings of a love of poetry in me simply by asking us to learn *off by heart* – an appropriate phrase – certain poems. Lines from some of those poems left an indelible mark on my mind. Among my favourites was *Nod* by Walter de la Mare. I took delight in the sheer musical sounds of the words. I particularly loved the beautiful and moving last verse of this poem even if I did not fully understand it:

> *His are the quiet steeps of dreamland,*
> *The waters of no-more-pain,*
> *His ram's bell rings 'neath an arch of stars,*
> *'Rest, rest, and rest again.'*

Another poem by Walter de la Mare which I was moved by was a poem about an old donkey, called *Nicholas Nye*, which had been put out to grass after its useful life had come to an end. As with the old shepherd, *Nod*, the sad, dreamy tone of the poem instinctively appealed to me. Perhaps I had been handed down that Celtic melancholy from my paternal grandmother who had been born and brought up on the Isle of Skye although I had always associated her more with wilfulness than melancholy. However, I suspect that in her old age, my grandmother, frightened of being abandoned when the last of her family had left, could have related to this old donkey left to face the deepening dusk alone:

> *But dusk would come in the apple boughs,*
> *The green of the glow-worm shine,*
> *The birds in nest would crouch to rest,*
> *And home I'd trudge to mine;*
> *And there, in the moonlight, dark with dew,*
> *Asking not wherefore nor why,*
> *Would brood like a ghost, and as still as a post,*
> *Old Nicholas Nye.*

A poem which also appealed to me deeply was called *The Vagabond* by Robert Louis Stevenson. There was a part of me that longed to escape into an imagined freedom. To escape from the constrictions of childhood and to grow up is so often to exchange one imprisoning routine for another. Although I did not dislike school, part of me wanted to break free of the daily routine of rising early, washing, having breakfast, going to school and waiting for the bell to ring at 4 o'clock, go home, have tea, then later go to bed and do it all over again the next day. Perhaps an underlying reason as to why I threw stones at the tinker's tent was that I envied them their apparent freedom from society's constraining norms. I envied the life of *The Vagabond*:

> *Give to me the life I love,*
> *Let the lave go by me,*
> *Give the jolly heaven above*
> *And the byway nigh me.*
> *Bed in the bush with stars to see,*
> *Bread I dip in the river –*
> *There's the life for a man like me,*
> *There's the life for ever.*

I loved that line: *Bread I dip in the river* with all its connotations of the simple, seemingly carefree life which did not involve working from 8 to 5 and having to go down to the shop at Port Askaig with a shopping bag every Saturday morning. In poetry, I found that others had shared some of my secret longings and they reminded me that I wasn't entirely alone.

CHAPTER 21

Taking to the Stage

There were two highlights of the school year and one was the play we put on for the benefit of our parents each December. This short play which was staged in the school dining-room seemed to require endless rehearsals. Although performing in public is not something which comes naturally to me, I rather enjoyed standing on the makeshift stage and spouting my few lines, if only to show off how well I was able to remember them. I found that I was able, to a small extent, to hide behind the character I was supposed to be enacting – not that I was ever much of an actor or that any acting talent was required to take part. Given the number of pupils in the Big Room, a part of sorts, however small, was given to everyone. From autumn onwards, we used to run through this play, some struggling to learn their lines more than others. It was something every pupil appeared to enjoy and, if nothing else, it provided a break from listening to *Squeak* droning on about how to parse a sentence or list the many and various exports of British Columbia.

Precisely because he knew that every, or almost every, pupil enjoyed the annual play, *Squeak* would continually threaten to abandon it if there was any sign of misbehaviour or lack of attention to any of the other subjects. Every year, we would go through the *definite* cancellations between October and the great day of the play in December. Of course, we knew that, despite all the cancellations, the play would go ahead as originally planned as it did every year. Although I spent many hours learning my lines, I can only now vaguely remember one of the four plays in which I took part. It involved a principal character who was constantly boasting about his virtues and achievements and reminded me of my Uncle Isaac. I was not given this leading role; I believe that it was played by the headteacher's younger son.

There were only three occasions in the year in which my parents travelled by taxi: the school play, the school Christmas party and the annual show which was held on the machair of Loch Indaal, outside Bridgend. The first two great events of each year were only attended by my mother as even in winter, my father would have the reason, or the excuse, not to join us as he had the Big House boiler to attend to or he had to check the heating in the greenhouses. On the opening, and only, night of the play, I'd walk nervously into the crowded school dining-room, hearing the adult voices echoing beneath the low ceiling and make my way up on to the wooden stage and stand concealed behind one side of the curtain and await my turn to move to the front of the stage with its imaginary footlights. I delivered my few lines as loudly as I dared. Perhaps it was fortunate that the plays were of a comic nature as if the audience laughed, I could reassure myself that they were laughing at the play and not at me.

The second highlight of the school year was the Christmas party which was also held in the school dining-room. I looked forward to that with less nervousness as I did not have to go on the stage. After a while, I'd begin to relax a little at the party and enjoy the rare treat of ice-cream and jelly. The tall Christmas tree stood with its glowing lights in the corner of the dining-room – almost all social events took place in that dining-room – with the curtains drawn against the darkness and, usually, the wind and rain of an Islay winter. There would be the songs such as *Rudolph the Red Nose Reindeer* and *Good King Wenceslas* which I would do my best to join in although I was no singer, as *Squeak* commented on more than once. Best of all was the moment near the end of the evening when the lights were dimmed and through the door stepped Santa Claus with his stuck-on white beard to hand out the presents. Just before his entrance, it was announced that a sleigh had just stopped outside the school. I awaited the calling of my name and then stepped across the varnished floor to receive my present. I later learned that Santa had not come all the way from the North Pole but from Caol Ila where his main job was working at the distillery. One of the girls once said to Santa that he looked so like her grandfather and he was!

When the evening finally ended, my mother, George and I waited on the school steps for MacIndeor's taxi to take us home. I felt an excitement about being driven in the winter darkness along the road I so often walked. I felt my usual sense of fear as the car went down the steep brae and around the sharp corner above Port Askaig. If the brakes should fail, all that could prevent us from falling down the high cliff to the sea, or on to the concrete pier below us, was a low wall. Having safely negotiated the bend one more time, the cattle grid rattled as we were driven across it and the headlights revealed the arch of bare trees over the drive; often a shower of raindrops fell on the roof of the car. It was as though we had entered a tunnel until we came to the Big House where only the window of the housekeeper's parlour was lit, casting an oblong of light on the lawn. As I stepped out of the car, the rush of waves could be heard and outside our house the lit windows of the lonely house across the Sound on Jura shone out in the darkness like a beacon. As it was Christmas, a fire was lit in the front room, casting altering shapes of shadows across the ceiling.

CHAPTER 22

Visitors

There were some regular visitors which broke the monotony of my mother's days when the children were at school, or in the case of Isabel, had left home as soon as she could to go to the imagined world of the mainland, or when my father was working all hours in the garden or mowing the front and back lawns of the Big House, or working on the drive.

There was Donnie the Post, who, from time to time, brought letters from her family in the Borders. There was the *Co-op* van which came across each Friday afternoon with a small range of groceries. In another of her attempts to speak posh, my mother would say *Thank o grocer* at the end of her shopping. Although she would never shop at Port Askaig store, she would look forward to the coming of the van and might even take off her pinny in honour of the occasion.

There was the woman nicknamed *Lily Fish* who came around in a small van selling a range of fish. Lily was a woman of many talents: a bagpipe player, a photographer, a poet of sorts, and a hairdresser – she often boasted of trimming the sparse locks of Helmut Schroder. She was an enterprising lady who turned a shed, close to her house, situated just above the shore at Caol Ila, into a sweet shop, with varying opening hours. She had an unusual affinity with the natural world and said that she liked to listen to the gulls talking to the seals. She had a brother who was known as *Willy Fish*.

There was the farmer who brought around a dozen eggs or so every second Saturday evening. As was the custom, he was named after his farm, *Balulive*. He was a curiously shaped man with long, thin legs, emphasized by the narrow legged trousers he wore which didn't quite reach his ankles, and a top-heavy body. I found myself wondering that if he had a fall, how on earth would anyone be able to get him upright again. After handing over the eggs, he would stay for hours to have a good blether, with a large sprinkling of not so harmless gossip which he enjoyed as much as my parents. His farm was situated miles from anywhere up a single-track road, crested with grass, past the turn off to Finlaggan Loch and the ruins of the castle of the Lords of the Isles which, like all such historical landmarks on the island at time, was largely unmarked: its stone symbols of ambition, power and wealth left to merge back into the land from which they came. Finlaggan is now a visitor centre.

The gamekeeper's assistant, when he wasn't swinging cats by their tails, would visit more frequently when he began to court my sister, Catherine. Despite his cruelty to cats, I rather liked his cheerfulness and his quirky way of looking at the world. In his seeming indifference to the suffering of animals, he was perhaps closer to the natural world than I was.

The most memorable of the occasional visitors was a Pakistani salesman who arrived at our door on his bike, on the rear rack of which he somehow balanced a large, leather suitcase. He would lean his bike against the wall of our porch and take off the heavy suitcase and loudly knock at the door. When my mother opened the door and saw the man standing there with the suitcase at his feet, she felt obliged to invite him in. He would lift the case on to the kitchen table, open the clasps and proceed to remove item after item from his seemingly bottomless suitcase: dresses, scarves, blouses, head squares, hankies, tea towels, pinnies, vests and so on. He reminded me of magicians I had seen on television removing hanky after hanky, strung together, from their pockets or an unending stream of ping pong balls from their mouths. I was always struck by the man's wonderful persistence and cheerfulness. No matter how many items my mother rejected, he would continue smiling. When all else failed, he would bring out and hold up to the light a pair of large bloomers which he called *neekers: please madam, look at those lovely neekers.* He took the view that no lady can ever possess too many pairs of knickers. Sometimes, on the few occasions when she had cash in her purse which had not already been earmarked for something more essential, my mother would relent and buy an item or two, whether it was *neekers* or a tea towel. Even if he sold nothing, he simply performed the amazing feat of returning all the countless items back into his suitcase and lift it on to the back of his bike and try his luck next door and further up the drive to Granny Chisholm who, even if she did not buy anything, would offer him a cup of tea and a biscuit which had long since lost its crispness.

It never occurred to us to wonder where this Pakistani man came from or how many miles he had cycled, or what he did in the many days of gales and rain. Where did he spend each night on the island given that he seemed to sell so little, would he not have spent more money on a B&B than he made from sales? Those were questions we never asked. He was just someone who appeared from time to time, seemingly out of nowhere and returned to the nowhere from which he had come.

Most of the clothes my mother bought were from the various mail order catalogues which came through the post as there was no shop which sold reasonably priced clothes on the island. The three catalogues my mother used were *JD Williams, Marshall Ward* and *Fairfords. JD Williams* was the superior one and the most expensive of the three and she could only afford to buy clothes from there when the family finances were less limited than usual. There were one or two shops on the island which sold clothes but they were well beyond my family's price range as they catered for affluent tourists. My father was paid fortnightly and the weeks in which my father was not paid were called *blin* weeks by my mother. During *blin* weeks, she was reduced to buying from *Fairfords* which was the catalogue equivalent to today's *Primark*. Clothes from *Fairfords* were cheap and of low quality with a tendency to shrink in the wash. It also took up to a month before they got around to sending the order. Of course, most of the clothes I wore were handed down from my brother. Whenever a parcel arrived at our door in any way damaged, my mother would suspect the wife of the post office owner at Port Askaig of taking a *peek* at what she had bought. She was inclined to paranoia and mistrusted almost everyone who was outside her family – not that she had complete trust in them. She had a suspicion about strangers and nearly all the visitors to our house were drawn there by my more sociable father. Indeed, some visitors would come straight to the garden rather than risk my mother's moods.

A regular visitor to the garden was the retired estate gamekeeper called Mr Frazer who was a gentle man – I could not imagine him actually killing anything. He spoke softly and his face was nearly always obscured behind the thick smoke of his pipe. I liked the way in which he took out the tin printed with the romantic sounding name of *Golden Virginia Coarse Cut* from his waistcoat pocket. He would tap the tobacco into the bowl of his curved pipe and then hold a match to it and puff vigorously to get it going to his satisfaction. Smoke rose slowly in circles and a trail of vanilla scent pervaded the air. It was the influence of Mr Frazer and the episodes of *Maigret* which I watched on television that encouraged me in my mid-teens to send off for a pipe, unknown to my mother, through a catalogue. After a few puffs, I had rarely felt so ill and if I had viewed myself in a mirror, I expect that I would have been shocked by the greenness of my face. I thought that smoking a pipe would make me appear mysterious and wise but it only made me nauseous.

Each year, Frazer entered a miniature house and garden into the plant and produce competition in the Islay Show. He and my father spent hours together in the coolness and gloom of the top potting shed creating the idyllic world of a wooden house with its green painted door and shuttered windows, surrounded by a garden, enclosed by a matchstick wicker fence painted white, where cuttings of shrubs were trees and lawns were made of moss with islands of tiny flower beds. It was a world in which the invisible, imaginary family who lived within never quarrelled or shouted at each other in anger and frustration. I found myself longing to live in that world but I was much too large to enter.

Other visitors to the potting shed in which a paraffin stove cast shadows across the peeling, distempered walls were the bereaved or the friends of the deceased who came to ask my father to make a wreath. When I was a little older, it was my job to go in search of moss in the surrounding woodlands. In the mild, wet climate of Islay, moss grows in abundance. One of the best places to gather moss was to walk along the path just down from Granny Chisholm's house. This path leads to a gate which opens on to moorland and there is a steep, slippery track which takes you down to the small lighthouse. It was on the pier of that lighthouse where one evening as dusk was descending, I caught a strange, orange coloured fish which dropped from my hook just as I was about to land it. Many times, I have wondered what I may have caught if only I could have kept hold of it. Losing that fish was like a beautiful dream which dissolves on waking.

From the sides of this path and around the trunks of the trees, I pulled up handful after handful of the moss, trying to avoid gathering twigs and weeds. Rainwater from the moss trickled through my fingers as I squeezed it. Eventually, I filled the hessian sack and returned to the potting shed where my father had paused from his work to draw on a *Capstan* cigarette, the smoke slowly drifting into the air. I would watch my father as he twisted wire into a ring and then bind the moss tightly around it. He had served a full apprenticeship in gardening and he had been taught to master every aspect of the craft. When both ends of the mossed circle met, like the joining of hands in marriage, he twisted wire around the flowers and foliage and then pressed each one into the soft bed of moss to create something ornate and colourful: out of grief arose beauty.

There was a mother and daughter from Portnahaven who visited our house and the garden some Sundays. The daughter was a tall, thin lady with a kind, smiling face. She was one of my favourite visitors as she always brought sweets for myself and George. I was told by my father that these women belonged to a strange and strict sect called the Plymouth Brethren. They must have felt rather isolated on the island where, as far as I knew, no one else belonged to that sect. Those visits to Dunlossit may have been a welcome break for the mother in particular; her daughter was a teacher at Bowmore Secondary. The day I would have to leave Keills Primary and get the bus to Bowmore each day was fast approaching, a prospect I rather dreaded. To move from a school with under thirty pupils to a school of some three hundred seemed such a daunting prospect for someone like myself who disliked crowds, partly because I had no experience of them.

There were of course the regular visits to the garden by the estate factor, Mr MacCrae, who was regarded by my mother as a class above and therefore to be envied and mistrusted. He dressed in a tweed suit and tie and his shoes were invariably polished so he was different from almost every other man we encountered. His wife was also a rather superior lady or, to use my mother's words about her, *stuck up*. She and her husband lived in a large house with a long drive outside Ballygrant, just out of reach of the limestone quarry from where explosions could occasionally be heard when the rock was blasted and clouds of dust rose into the air and slowly descended, covering everything within a radius of a few hundred yards in a white film, like fallen snow. Our next-door neighbour, Donny Chisholm worked in the quarry and had done so for many years. When I heard him cough, splutter and wheeze when he tried to talk, I gather that much of this dust must have formed a thick coating on his lungs. I was told that he was a skilful footballer in his younger days and would fly down the wing with the ball at his feet but like so many who worked in estate sawmills and quarries, little care was taken for the health of the workers.

Those regular visitors to our house and the garden added a much-needed element of variation to our routine when days would otherwise merge seamlessly into each other. Looking back on the characters who peopled my childhood, they seemed to have a surreal quality, an individuality which has been partly lost, due to the standardisation brought about by mass culture. It's as though people in that time and in that place had more freedom to be themselves.

CHAPTER 23

Chalk Dust and Golden Wrappers

After three years in the Big Room at Keills, I finally made my journey across the rows of desks, to sit at the back of the class, nearest to the wide window. I was now in Primary 7 and on my final year in that school with its view down across the field to the woodlands of Dunlossit; beyond the trees, the Sound of Islay and beyond the sea, the russet slopes of Jura. On some mornings, the sea and the slopes were obscured by mist as if they had been rubbed out on the page of a jotter. On other mornings, the sea glowed as if with a light of its own making. The tendency to gaze out of the window and daydream only intensified as I got older. I still gazed at the crows, their feathers shifting on the stone wall, as I did when I was in the Wee Room but my longings for something other increased.

I now gazed admiringly at one or two of the girls in the room – there were no girls in Primary 7, just three other boys. There was a girl a year or two younger than myself called Valerie who had long, dark hair who I admired from afar. I once walked part of my way to school with her and she gave me a *Quality Street* toffee with its golden wrapper. I kept it in my blazer pocket for weeks as I regarded it as being too precious to eat. I only finally got rid of the toffee when it became soft and stuck to the inner lining of my pocket. I naturally took this gift as a token of her affection for me but, in retrospect, it may be simply that she preferred soft centres. Valerie being one of the few girls in the Big Room had no shortage of admirers so I felt that I stood little chance with her but that only served to increase my longing.

There was a girl who joined my class in the previous year but her parents only stayed on the island for a short period. Her name was Barbara and she came from an exotic sounding place on the mainland called Kirkintilloch. Barbara was a rather superior girl and was unique among pupils in the school in being studious. In every test, she would come first and put myself and other members of my class to shame. She had long, light brown hair and a sweet, freckled face. She was a serious girl and even at the age of eleven had developed a manner of looking down on those she considered to be her inferiors. She seemed not to indulge in the childish games of the other girls at playtime. I felt drawn to her air of distance but, like so many of my dreams, they came to nothing. She left the school as suddenly as she had appeared but over the years, her image has come into my mind in the mysterious way in which faces of the past do. I find myself wondering whatever became of her when she presumably returned to the mainland which I had only once set foot on and the journey there had come so close to costing me my life.

Another girl who I admired was called Sheila. She had blonde hair which caught the sunlight which, from time to time, would stream through the side window. Although she sat on the desk next to mine, we rarely spoke, partly because boys and girls, on the whole, kept their distance and partly because I was too shy to talk to her. The more I admired a girl, the more hesitant I was to speak to her. I was crippled by a fear of rejection and being made fun of. All those childish 'love affairs' of mine existed only in my mind and perhaps it is partly because of that, that they have stayed with me as they remain untainted by reality. To this day, those once adored faces emerge from my past out of nowhere. It's as if our minds are crowded with people we once knew, many still living, but some now dead; each live on in the depth of our memories to rise to the surface at the least expected times due to some trigger in the mind which we cannot control. It is in that sense that the dead do not die for us as long as we ourselves live. With images of chalk dust falling to the varnished floor on those long afternoons in the Big Room, with the wind against the wide window muffling *Squeak's* voice as he droned on about fractions which he wrote on the smudged blackboard, the faces of Valerie, Barbara and Sheila loom out of my memory in which they reside. And it is not just certain girls which live on in my memory but many of the other pupils in that small, enclosed world of the Big Room, their names still echo through my mind: Billy, Innes, Neil, Donald James, Duncan, Jocky, Ann, Francis, Graham, Peter and Frazer who, like Sandy, had learning difficulties and whose father once forced him to enter the school by threatening him with a thick, leather belt. Certain images, like certain people, became permanent lodgers in one's mind and cannot be evicted.

I remember my very last day as a pupil at Keills. Myself and my three classmates, Billy, Innes and Neil, sat on the tarmac at the front of the school, our backs leaning against the white, pebble-dashed wall beneath the dining-hall windows and looked down across the fields and over the line of trees to the sea which shimmered in the June sunlight. It was one of those clear days when we could see all the way up the Sound. On the fence across the road, crows with their all-seeing eyes were perched, their tail feathers barely moving in the gentle breeze. We could hear the faint bleating of sheep as they grazed on the conical hills above the village. Black cattle with white patches on their flanks stood near the farmyard, slowly swinging their tails as if beating time to music only they could hear. At spaced intervals, a car or a lorry would pass along the road to or from Port Askaig to momentarily disturb the sense of stillness. We sensed that we had reached a turning point in our lives and nothing would ever be quite the same again. As with so many turning points, we approached it with feelings of anticipation and fear.

This school had been our second home for the past seven years, much more than half our lives. My life had been largely confined to a square mile: from Dunlossit to Port Askaig, to Keills and to Caol Ila for Sunday school. Our family walk on dry Sunday afternoons was to Loch Allan which lay within the line of trees I looked down on from where I sat. It was only on a few occasions that I ventured beyond that enclosed world in which I knew every field, every tree, every yard of road which I so often walked, morning and afternoon. Even now, that square mile is the only place which feels wholly permanent and real to me, the only area in which I feel at home. Everywhere else I have lived I have been a stranger just passing through. Much as I love Islay, my island in many respects consists of that one square mile. When I return to other places on Islay: Bowmore, Port Ellen, Port

Charlotte, Portnahaven and so on, I am re-visiting but when I get to Port Askaig, Caol Ila, Keills and, above all, Dunlossit, I have come home.

On the afternoon of that final day, I sat at my desk in the corner and looked around me at the four rows of desks which I had traversed over the years. There was Sandy still bent over his dog-eared jotter, drawing smudged circles around his penny, drawing clock hands with his own too large hands. *Squeak* with his unkempt beard was at the blackboard with his worn-out piece of chalk which, from time to time, made a squealing noise that pierced through my daydreaming. Through the window, the grass of the playground lengthened in the soft summer breeze.

The minute hand of the walled classroom clock moved closer and closer to 4 o'clock and for once, *Squeak* did not keep us in longer. I remembered the time when the manager of Caol Ila distillery arrived to take his two children home for lunch. He became impatient sitting in his car long after the bell should have rung. He came into the school and knocked on the door of the Big Room, demanding to know why the pupils had not been allowed to leave. When *Squeak* was confronted by someone he regarded as his social superior, he had a curious way of rubbing his hands together and bowing and simpering, rather like Uriah Heap in *David Copperfield* which I had seen on television. On this my final day, there was no delay and no simpering. I walked out of that classroom never to return although there have been times when I have longed to sit once more at that desk with its well encircled with ink from the many times I dipped my wood stemmed pen with its sharp metal tip, like all those pupils before me, and formed copperplate letters between the faint blue lines on the jotter. Although that classroom with its maps pinned to the wall was often a place of boredom, it was also a place of comforting routine. I am struck by the irony that so often when I sat at my desk and longed to escape for something more, after I left, I found myself sometimes longing to return. It's so difficult to live in the present moment.

I followed the others out of the classroom, along the corridor with its echoing footsteps, out of the back door into the sunlight. The cattle who were munching the lush grass in the field behind the playground fence, raised their heads momentarily as we passed before resuming their munching. Although the daunting first day at Bowmore Secondary awaited me, before that there was the long summer holiday to look forward to. Two months of relative freedom lay in front of me, what the children in Enid Blyton's *Famous Five* called the *hols* in which they would embark on some adventure which never seemed to happen to me.

CHAPTER 24

Long Summer Evenings and Polythene Bags

George and I had only a few playmates during the long school summer holidays, apart from Duncan and Donald James. We would play endless games of football in the yard across from our house. On the occasions when I watched football on television through the snowstorm, I was entranced by watching the great Real Madrid team of the 1960s and as I kicked the ball around the yard, I imagined myself as Gento or Di Stefano and pretended that I heard the roar of the crowd each time I scored a goal. Given that my father was a lifelong Rangers supporter and almost all the people I knew on Islay supported Rangers, whether or not they had ever set foot inside Ibrox Park, I too became a follower and when I was not fantasizing about playing for the world's greatest team, I would imagine myself racing down the wing, dribbling past three defenders as I saw Willie Henderson do on *Sportsreel*. When we played football late into the summer evening, we would switch on the single wall light in the yard and pretend we were playing under floodlights.

On still summer evenings when drizzle settled on the leaves of the sycamores, the midges were so ferocious that my brother and I pulled a clear polythene bag over our heads to reduce the bites on our head, neck and ears even at the risk of suffocation. With our faces obscured by the misted polythene, we must have looked rather like astronauts about to step on to the moon. Apart from the risk and discomfort of the polythene bag, the only other partial remedy was to smear our faces with a thick, sticky paste which came in a round tin. I dread to think what ingredients were in this chemical concoction but it stung my skin and was almost entirely ineffective in keeping the midges at bay. My father used to smear this paste over his face and bare arms, particularly when he was scything and had no free hand with which to scratch. I think that the fact the paste stung so much, convinced him that it was doing some good. I can see him now swinging his scythe across a bank of long, wet grass with a halo of midges around his frizzy, greying hair with the only partial relief from the biting, made by a stray breeze rising from the sea which momentarily cleared the halo around his head.

On evenings when not playing football, we took our fishing rods, which were sawn lengths of hazel on which was wound an orange fishing line with a hook attached, down to the Wee Pier below our house. We went down the slippery, mossed steps through the narrow opening in the wooded cliff, bordered with wild garlic, which we called Midge Alley for here the midges congregated in thick clouds. Even in summer, those steps dripped with water and with the constant moisture and the shelter, the midges must have thought they had found their heaven. Having negotiated that torturous tunnel, it was with relief we reached the opening to the shore where rocks were stuck with limpets; cockles, and empty razor clam shells were littered between the rocks and sometimes jelly fish lay dead, their translucent flesh coloured by a stray glimpse of evening sunlight. We walked along to the end of the pier which jutted out into the Sound, its bouldered sides broken by years of storms. Sometimes a cargo ship passed, its long, low deck laden with wood and in its wake, waves washed against the shore, darkening the dried rocks with spray and formed eddies around the pier on which we stood. When I stood on the pier at Port Askaig when the *Lochiel* left, I experienced the sensation that it was not the ferry which was moving but the pier and I was being taken away to somewhere else I could only imagine. Some evenings, the *MacBraynes* cargo ship, the *Loch Ard*, passed on its way to or from Caol Ila or Bunnahabhain distillery. Each distillery on the island had its own pier and the barrels of whisky would be loaded on to the ship to be taken to warehouses near Glasgow. Now the narrow island roads are eroded and made dangerous by massive tankers taking the whisky to the roll on and off ferries. Due to the relentless increase in traffic, the once peaceful hamlet of Port Askaig – apart from when the ferry arrived – has been despoiled through development; so many of its beautiful ash trees cut down. Islay has lost the quietness which it had when I was a child. It's as if the spaces of silence have been filled.

We rarely caught anything as we stood on that narrow pier apart from strands of seaweed and more midge bites. Occasionally, I felt the chug on my hazel stick and I glimpsed the orange line circling below the surface of the sea. I raised the rod and saw a small, slate grey fish wriggle on the hook. I felt a thrill when I felt that tug on the rod but I hated removing the hook from the struggling fish's mouth which would bleed a little. I looked down on the fish gasping with its open mouth. I do not know why I did not return those fish to the sea. I suppose I regarded them as small trophies to show that my fishing expedition was not a complete waste of time. I carried the fish back up the steps, trying to avoid looking at the overhanging rock in which the avenging ghost of the sheep might lurk. When I had no fish to take home with me, I felt a sense of disappointment and when I did, I felt a sense of guilt at more needless killing.

CHAPTER 25

The Allure of the Dark

Some afternoons, George and I, and sometimes the MacPhee brothers, took the boat out on Loch Allan. Instead of following the drive which went up past the yard, we walked up the muddy path behind the back wall of the garden. This path rarely, if ever, dried out and I slipped and slid on the mud with my often leaking wellies – my father's attempts to patch them with the bicycle repair kit were never wholly successful.

At the top of this steep path, stood the large tank with a rusty tin roof which supplied the Big House and others with water. It was another task of my father's to check the water level in this tank. He would turn the key he kept under a stone outside the tank to unlock the rusty padlock and when the door was open, it let in a shaft of light across the still, dark surface of the water. After long periods of rain – not an infrequent occurrence on Islay – the level of the water would be just a few inches from the door. I remember how frightened I was when I first looked into that tank by its deep darkness. It was as if I was looking into the face of death. From time to time, I would have terrible dreams about being accidentally locked in this tank, being left to cling on to the back of the door until my fingers grew cold and numb and I could hold on no longer and drop into the water, my screams and my splashes unheard. Even when I return to Islay and follow that same muddy path to the tank, wearing wellies which no longer leak, I feel the return of that old childish fear. The many fears of childhood never completely dissolve, we just learn to keep them beneath our conscious mind, never knowing what sight, touch, taste, sound, or scent will bring them looming once more to the surface.

Close to the tank was a pond which was always referred to as the Black Loch. This pond had the same still, dark surface as the water in the tank. It was surrounded by trees with lichened branches and rhododendrons which sunlight rarely penetrated. As the opened door of the tank would cast a frail light across the darkness, sometimes a shadow would move across the pond when the clouds shifted. The Black Loch as the name implies had an air of mystery about it. Given my fears of the water tank and the pond, you may wonder why I ever took this shortcut but there is a certain thrill in confronting one's fears, particularly as a child. Although, even now, I would be reluctant to walk up that narrow path on my own as night comes on.

When we eventually reached the end of this supposed shortcut – I find that shortcuts rarely live up to their name – we were on the drive which led past the loch on which lily pads join hands across the surface and open their bowls to gather sunlight in summer. Loch Allan, at that time, was hidden from the drive and you had to walk through an arch of evergreens to reach it. The boathouse, thatched with heather, dipped its toes in to the loch and when you opened the door, you could see and hear the wavelets lapping through the slatted boards beneath your feet. There was a small window in the boathouse through which you would invariably glimpse a pair of mute swans gliding around a bay, sometimes dipping their elegant necks below the surface in search of weeds. On days when the surface of the loch was still, concentric circles of water could be seen after each dip. Even with the window and the boathouse door opened to let in the light of summer, there was a gloom and coolness within which I liked. In the moment when we stopped talking, all that I could hear would be the gentle licking of water against the stanchions and against the varnished gunwales of the wooden boat which lay beneath the planks of the floor. The boat rising and falling with the motion of the water as if it measured its own time which had slowed.

The boat was tied with a length of coarse rope to a metal ring on the wall. The oars lay like resting arms on the seats. The gamekeeper always removed the rollocks to stop people like us from taking it out without permission and without payment. However, this lack of rollocks did not stop us and one of us would stand up and use one of the oars rather as if we were punting.

George usually took the responsibility, as he did in most matters, to move the boat out by levering an oar against the side of the boathouse. When the water became too deep to punt, he stood at the stern and dipped the oar in and out of the water to propel us. In the middle of the loch, the boat was left to drift with the breeze so that we could glide and trail a fishing line behind us. Sometimes, we caught a tiny brown trout with mottled markings, too small to eat. More than the pleasure of catching a fish, I loved the feeling of being cast adrift, lying back and dipping my fingers into the water which was chilly even in summer. I leaned over the side and gazed down into the peated depths. As the boat drifted into a bay, we sometimes disturbed the swans who paddled away from us, appearing indignant at being disturbed by intruders in their settled world. As the boat came closer to the shallows around the shore, George manned an oar and pushed against a rock to stop us from running aground.

On the far side of Loch Allan was a steep weir and there was always a fear that a strong wind would arise suddenly, as it often did on Islay, and push the boat closer and closer to the edge, particularly when the loch was high after days of heavy rain. We would be powerless to prevent the boat from going over and falling as if over the rim of our world. The weir was steep and beneath was a rapidly flowing river which rushed through the trees before descending in a waterfall, then flowing out into the sea or into a channel which led into the turbine house. It was the power of this river which generated electricity. Whenever the boat drifted close to the weir, I felt this frisson of fear. Like many children, particularly boys, there was this desire to take risks as there was an element of pleasure in feeling afraid. A small part of me would have liked the boat to go over and down, to what I referred to as the rapids, having watched too many cowboy films on television, just to experience what it felt like. Like almost all island children at that time, I had no idea how to swim, and that in a perverse sense added to my sense of adventure. We would dare each other to take risks. In order to impress my peers: I climbed across the high rocks near the Wee Pier when the tide was in, knowing that if I slipped and fell, I would be in danger of drowning. I climbed high into a tree and risked falling from a breaking branch. One of our favourite games was sitting on top of the garden wall and jump, then move across to a higher part of the wall and jump again to find out who could leap from the highest height.

There was a deeper part of me which lay beyond the showing off, which wondered what it would be like to jump off a high cliff, knowing that the result would be certain death: that imagined feeling of falling and falling, as if flying, through currents of air into something beyond all my imagining. Below our house, there was a mossy path which led to the white bridge, below which were the steep steps to the Wee Pier. Halfway along the path, was a long, sheer drop to the rocks below. In my early years, this dangerous drop was not fenced and if you were not careful, it would be possible to slip on the often, muddy path and, unless you grasped hold of a gorse bush or rhododendron, you would fall to your death below. To walk along this path in darkness in our world far removed from street lights would be especially dangerous. I sometimes stood on the very edge of this path and gazed down. From where I stood, I could not see the rocks which I knew were there below me, all I could see and hear were the waves and I felt this curious temptation to jump. It was as if an inner voice was daring me. It was not because I was in the depths of despair or wanted to end my life, it was just this desire to experience what I imagined to be moments of complete exhilaration. It was as if such moments were worth more than a lifetime of cautious routine.

Of course, a child has a different perception of death than an adult, particularly an adult who has moved closer to the end of his expected life span. In my childish mind, I could not grasp the seeming finality of it, there was a part of me which expected to return from my experience of falling. Many years later, I remember walking through a graveyard with a young child when we came across a newly erected headstone. I told the child that I knew the person whose name was engraved on the stone, and she told me that if that was her, she would be able to lift the stone and get out. She simply could not grasp the concept of death: for her, there was always a way out. One can never fully enter the mind of one's childish self. The novelist LP Hartley said that *the past is a strange country* and our early mind is also a strange country. However, rather like this child, I always imagined that even when I died, I would somehow manage to find a way out and that death would not be the end of me. In this sense, perhaps all children up until a certain age believe themselves to be immortal. When the day arrives when you no longer believe that, you leave your childhood behind. In that respect, I have never entirely lost my belief in some form of immortality and perhaps that's why Christ was so welcoming of children or those who preserve the child within themselves. There is always the nagging doubt that I am deluding myself because I am too childish to confront oblivion, but the only way to avoid doubt in life is to avoid thought.

At the end of the afternoon on the loch, we managed by a combination of punting and propelling to get the boat back through the entrance of the boathouse – it usually took two or three attempts to achieve this. The dripping oars were laid to rest on the benches as if no one had touched them. We clambered out of the boat on to the wooden boards above, when the water level was low, sometimes getting a splinter on our bare knees. George, not trusting me, would tie the rope on to the ring as if he was tying a horse outside a saloon with its swinging doors. Through the window, I looked out and saw the swans gliding back around the bay now that the momentary disturbance in their world was over, their feathers sleeked back in place by their sides. They would continue to glide through the evening stillness with the last of the sun casting veils of light across the surface of the loch. We made our way back along the drive and above the yard, Donald James and Duncan would take the turning which led to the Gate Lodge and George and I would head down the drive towards home where our mother would be struggling to keep the meal hot on the *Wellstood* range which had a mind of its own. She would be cursing my father, who also had a mind of his own, for being late yet again.

CHAPTER 26

The Lost Coin

On days when our bikes were working – there so often seemed to be a problem with punctures and chains slipping off – we cycled as far as the furthest away loch on the back drive: Ballygrant Loch. We often had to wait for my father to get around to fixing the puncture with the repair kit he kept in a drawer in the scullery which we called the back kitchen where the stone sink was in which my mother washed all of the family's clothes by hand. After the rinsing, she'd wring out each piece of washing and place it in the wicker basket like a throttled snake. When he came to open the repair kit, there would be no patches or no glue, and we would have to wait until my mother's next shopping trip to Bowmore. My father's attempts at sticking a patch on an inner tube was often no more successful than his attempt to stick a patch on my wellies. So often when I went out on my bike, I would feel that sense of deflation when the rim of the tyre started bumping and rattling on the gravel. Still, possessing a bike extended the world for myself and George. I remember the thrill of anticipation which I experienced as I waited on the pier at Port – we never referred to it as Port Askaig since it was the only port in our lives. My father had been informed from the seller that my second-hand bike was to arrive on a certain date and when the great day arrived, I stood waiting by his side as the *Lochiel* drew up alongside the pier. I was seven years old and this was the best birthday present I have ever received. For some reason, I expected my bike to be winched out of the ship's hold in a net, rather like a car, and landed on the pier. I watched the winch rise and fall time and time again, carrying everything but my long-awaited bike. When I had almost given up all hope, I saw a man wheel a small, white-framed bike down the gangway. My father collected the bike and soon I was its proud possessor. After a few attempts and a few falls and scraped knees, I soon mastered the art of cycling and I was able to explore a little more of my island world.

I hardly ever cycled along the main road that climbed up the steep, winding brae from Port, not that the main road was all that busy in the 1960s when so few people owned a car or could afford to do so. Until my last year on Islay, it was always the back drive on which I cycled, sometimes cycling the three or four miles to Ballygrant Loch, my tyres bumping over the limestone gravel, splashing through puddles after a night of rain or raising whitish dust during dry periods, usually in the spring when the succession of low pressure areas from the Atlantic can cease for weeks at a time. The back drive was especially lovely in springtime when the mossy banks were lit by primroses like stars suddenly revealing themselves out of a dark blanket of sky. Islay is an island of primroses and nowhere on the island do they grow more profusely than on Dunlossit Estate.

Later in the spring, on the verges and banks along Ballygrant Loch, waves of bluebells appear, swaying in unison in the winds which whisper through the woodlands clothed in pale green, translucent leaves shot through by the sun. I would lean my bike against the drystane wall of the bridge which arched over a stream that flowed into the loch and look across the surface on which insects danced, to the boatshed whose windows appeared like eyes which looked back at me from beneath the trees which formed a canopy above it. In all my thirteen and a half years on Islay, I never set foot in that boatshed and the fact that it seemed out of reach gave it a kind of romance like an unattainable ideal, rather like the miniature worlds which the retired gamekeeper and my father created out of moss, plant cuttings and wood. There was an island on Ballygrant Loch which I was told was a crannog, a man-made island on which a family or families lived in the far distant past. They lived on the island in order to avoid being killed by wild animals or by their human enemies, the water of the loch creating a moat. I found it hard to imagine how they could survive the gales and dampness of an island winter with their food supply dwindling and spring still a long way off. Then there would be the midges, the clegs and the deer ticks of summer and autumn. We cannot enter the world of such early people as their perceptions and expectations of life would be so much different to our own. They would not have had all the demands which we now make on our lives and they would have been spared the discontent we feel when all our many demands are not met.

Being Islay, I would often get caught in the rain on my cycle rides and I would head for a fallen tree and shelter under the canopy of the torn up roots around which clung peaty soil like the roof of a mud hut. I leant my bike up against a tree which was still standing and get under the canopy and wait for the rain to stop. I stood with bent back and listened to the raindrops as they pattered on the leaves of the rhododendrons which spread their palms, with their bronzed undersides, like human fingers. In early summer, cuckoos call out to each other repeatedly, seeming to delight in the sound of their own voices and only pausing momentarily to listen to the sound of the echoes. There was the far-off call of a curlew with its note of longing for something lost and never to be found again. Sometimes, I was disturbed by a red deer which shook the bracken as it fled, having scented danger, making the fronds of ferns shake and let fall droplets of gathered rain. So, there I stood waiting and waiting, not knowing if it was a brief shower or if the rain was set in for the rest of the day. One time when I was crouched beneath a root canopy, I dug a hole with a stick and buried a threepenny bit which I had in my pocket. It was unusual for me to have a coin in my pocket as I usually spent every penny on sweets in the shop at Port every Saturday afternoon.

I had read of tales of buried treasure in *The Famous Five*, who always drank ginger beer and never *Irn-Bru*, and I felt the need to bury my own treasure and come back later to dig it up when my need for money was greater. So, I carefully placed the bronzed, twelve-sided coin in the hole I had made and covered it with dark mud and rotted leaves. I now had a secret which I would not share with anyone. When I returned to that fallen tree weeks later, I could not find the coin which I had so carefully buried. Perhaps I should have drawn a map on which X marked the spot. I kept returning again and again but still failed to find it. After a while, I even had difficulty in remembering under which tree I had buried it. Many years later, when I had returned to Islay on holiday, I searched again but the search became impossible as other trees had fallen and some of the fallen trees which were there in my childhood had been removed.

That lost coin has become for me a symbol of my lost childhood. No matter how hard you try, your childhood can never be recovered. Nonetheless, through writing, you can recover fragments which you try to piece together to form a whole. Memory is uncertain and images often come to mind when you least expect them, rather like moments of happiness. In Marcel Proust's great novel, R*emembrance Of Things Past*, it was the taste of tea and madeleine through which the writer recovered his long buried childhood. For me, it would perhaps be the taste of *Cremola Foam* diluted with tepid, peaty water and perhaps containing a few drowned midges which might bring back those childhood summers. I remember the sickly, bitter aftertaste of the drink. If not that, it might be the creamy taste of *McCowan's Highland Toffee* or the penny toffees with their green and white waxy wrappers which open the closed casement of my past. Moving away from my childhood addiction to sugar, it might be the feel of the coarse leaves of the blackcurrant bushes against my bare knees when I spent hours picking them in the summer holidays, holding a woven, wicker punnet in my hand, wishing that I could fill the punnet more quickly with the shiny black and red currants, along with the odd green one and a few leaves thrown in. Or it could be the memory of picking gooseberries whose prickly stems scratched my bare arms. Our father would give myself and George so many coins per pound or per punnet picked which we would save to spend at the Islay Show in August. I still feel, however irrationally, that if I could one day find that buried threepenny bit, I would recover part of my lost childhood self. It may be that many centuries from now when Dunlossit House has long since fallen into ruin, rather like so many other country mansions, and the estate so long tended has reverted to nature, some archaeologist attempting to dig up the past to see how people once lived, will come across my threepenny bit and wonder who put it there and why.

CHAPTER 27

Dawn Raids

My eldest sister, Isabel, left home to attend a secretarial course in Glasgow where she endured the fate of so many people who moved to the city from the Highlands and Islands: she was regarded as a *Teuchter*, someone who did not possess a brain between her ears but a lump of peat. At that time, there was little or no respect given to those who grew up in the Gaelic speaking parts of Scotland, not that my sister knew more than a few words of Gaelic. Even those islanders who did not speak that language, their English was imbued with the lilt of the ancient tongue. There is also an almost unbridgeable gulf between those who grew up surrounded by trees, hills and lochs and those who grew up surrounded by streets and houses and the constant roar of traffic.

Later Isabel got a job in a solicitors' office in Oban – *The Gateway to the Hebrides* – where she must have felt less of an alien. When Isabel left home, Catherine was left to endure the burden of her mother's demands. It was her job to chop logs, bring in the coal from the shed across the drive, do much of the housework and so much else. Later, she came to work full-time in the garden where she seemed to take some pleasure, if only because it was an escape from her mother.

It's hard to believe but even Muriel had a brief period when she also was put to 'work' in the garden but she would only perform tasks slowly, and if it did not involve any bending, or if it didn't endanger her finger nails. She did not like working on days when it was raining or too windy, as it spoiled her hair style. This was something of a disadvantage as almost all days on Islay are wet or windy or often both. Partly in order to avoid unkempt hair,

Muriel developed a curious way of walking which involved not bending her knees. She would bend forward from her waist and take short steps with rigid legs. It was as if she was constantly trying to duck under a fallen branch.

Another difficulty which Muriel had was getting out of her bed in the morning. In the spring, all of us had to take our turn in getting up at dawn and go up to the garden to scare the wood pigeons from eating the young and tender brassica plants. My father did not trust the netting or the criss-crosses of string with the silver, red and gold strips of foil hanging and fluttering in the wind, making sounds like the wings of wood pigeons brushing the translucent leaves of the trees. Being the youngest, I largely escaped this chore but on the rare mornings when I did succeed in getting out of bed with the pale purple light of dawn stealing through the worn and faded bedroom curtains, I rather liked the chill of the air against my face. There was a freshness about the world when it seemed that everyone else was still asleep. The Sound seemed to breathe more heavily, its surface touched by a light which was filtered by mist as if through net curtains. The grass was drenched by dewdrops which hung suspended on each blade. The stamens of the fuchsias drooped lower with the weight of moisture. The birds sang more loudly than usual. I walked up the drive with my father and we stepped through the door into the garden filled with the promise of the richness of growth to come. It was as if everything was reaching up to the light. There would be a few wood pigeons hovering above the netting and the gently moving foils as if in search for a gap in the netting which was stretched over the sprouts, cauliflowers, cabbages and calabrese with their tender, tempting leaves. As we approached, the birds rose into the air, beating their wings with the sound of snapping elastic and flying up into the trees to perch until they would have the opportunity to try again when the coast was clear, and the stillness of dawn had settled once more.

I do not recall Muriel ever disturbing the pigeons in their dawn raids, if it was up to her, they could have all they could eat so long as she could stay in bed. After her brief, unhelpful attempt at being a gardener, she obtained a job in the hotel at Port Askaig where the proprietress, Mrs Spiers, possessed the ability to do what no one had ever been able to do before or since: get

Muriel to work and arrive on time most days. I think that Muriel experienced a period of happiness working in that hotel which she was rarely to achieve again in her troubled life. Although she had her share of what my parents regarded as unsuitable boyfriends, as did Isabel and Catherine, who as mentioned previously, one of whose boyfriends was the under-keeper on the estate who whirled cats around his head, they were protected by the closeness of the island community and without that protection, Muriel was lost.

Whenever my sisters were late coming home from a night out, George was dispatched on his trusty old bike to look for them like an Indian scout scouring the terrain for hostile forces. There were a pair of spinster sisters who lived with their mother in a house on the brae which looked down on Port Askaig, in more ways than one. They willingly took on the role of the community's moral guardians and would look with disapproval at all romantic goings on of the island's youth, perhaps tinged with some regret over their own unspent youth. Their brother worked as a steward on the *Lochiel* and wore a white jacket, a white shirt and a black bow tie in those days when *MacBraynes'* ferries had restaurants with white linen tablecloths before that was all swept away by the introduction of greasy spoon cafes.

There was a muddy path which led through thick woodland above the Gate Lodge which had an air of gloom even in daylight. Further along this tunnel-like path was an iron cage in which three headstones stood, one in the shape of a Celtic cross whose stone arms had been broken. Rather like the water tank and the black loch, I had a certain fear of this cage. I felt that the cage was not so much to keep intruders out but to keep the dead in. I never walked along this path in the darkness even if it meant avoiding walking up the steep brae. One evening, Isabel and Catherine were walking along this path and a man jumped out at them from behind the cage. This ghostly apparition turned out to be a local youth prone to playing practical jokes but the moment of terror remained with my sisters and I doubt that they ever walked past the caged dead again in darkness, even though it was one of the few places which George could not search with his bike.

It was when working in Oban that Isabel met the man who was to become her husband. Although Jim came from Lossiemouth, situated on the

Moray Firth coast, the small trawler he worked on fished off the west coast and sold their catch at the market in Oban where his boat often moored at weekends. When my parents first met Jim, they were not altogether impressed by their daughter's choice of partner. Their rather hostile attitude was not helped by the language barrier. Jim spoke English but not as we knew it. The combination of Jim's broad accent, a subtle variation of the Buchan dialect, and his tendency to converse in a rapid mumble gave rise to a communication barrier and the rest of the family tended to avoid being left alone in a room with Jim when Isabel was not there to act as his interpreter. Listening to Jim was rather like watching a foreign language film without subtitles. Whereas many people become more incoherent with the effect of alcohol, in Jim's case, he talked more lucidly after a few glasses of *Bacardi* and *Coke*.

Of course, my parents' disapproval did nothing to deter the romance which soon led to marriage. My mother and father attended the wedding of Isabel and Jim in Oban and there is a photo of them at the wedding with my mother looking miserable. She would not have regarded any man who married her daughter, particularly at such a young age, as being at all suitable. When the couple came to stay with us during the summer holidays, she would get angry at Jim who would do what no one in our house had ever done before: watch television in the morning. He would spend hours watching the British Open golf on the television which was placed in the kitchen with my mother working and flustering around him. It would have been sensible to have the set in the front room, but to sit in that room when it wasn't the Christmas season would have been too radical a concept for my mother to grasp. Jim later took up playing golf but he found the walking involved rather off-putting. Mark Twain said that playing golf was a good walk spoiled but, for Jim, golf was a good game spoiled by a walk.

My parents slowly came to appreciate Jim's fundamental decency and realised that their daughter had made a wise choice of husband. Because of Isabel's early marriage, I found myself an uncle at the age of ten which I had mixed feelings about. My nephew, Brian, cried rather a lot but I didn't know if this was something all babies did or that his ability to squawk for so long and so frequently put him into a class of his own. One of the very few things which kept him quiet was to stick a dummy coated with rose hip syrup in his mouth. I rather enjoyed taking Brian in his pushchair up the drive, past the garden and up around Granny Chisholm's and he appeared to enjoy those outings as during them, he would often stop crying. He seemed to be soothed not only by the motion but by the bird song that so filled the Dunlossit air in spring and summer. Perhaps also he was soothed by the sound of the ever-flowing tide which created a background music to our walks. Brian seemed amused by the fussing and clucking of the hens around the hen house in a clearing between the fuchsia bushes and the rowan trees down from Granny Chisholm's old house. The hens would claw at the mud and peck at the worms which were reluctantly exposed to the light. I had been told, on not very reliable authority, that if you fed rowan berries to hens, they would eat them and stagger around as if they were drunk. I tried this several times, partly to amuse Brian, but much to my disappointment, I never knew it to work. Still, I rather enjoyed those walks pushing the pram, it made a change from riding my imaginary horse with my pistol by my side in case I should come across Red Indians or surly looking cowboys up to no good.

CHAPTER 28

Wood Shavings and Knots

The day I dreaded arrived too soon. The summer holidays had ended and I found myself walking down the drive that August with George to get the school bus which would take me to Bowmore Secondary. I felt the coarse material of the long flannel trousers rub against my legs – I had never worn long trousers before. My woollen, navy blue blazer, bought at considerable expense by my parents, also felt restricting. We waited outside the Lodge gates and I saw the bus go down to the pier and turn before stopping to pick us up on the way back. The bus engine revved up the steep, winding brae which I had so often walked on my way to Keills Primary, past the Caol Ila road end and on the other side of the road, the gate where I had stood and watched my mother being chased by the bull some five years earlier. The gorse bushes were still in bloom but they had lost the dazzling yellow which they had in the spring. The bus stopped at the road end and a few children got on. I took a little comfort from seeing the face of Billy, my classmate at Keills, who was also enduring his first day at Bowmore. As the bus moved down the brae, I looked out at the burn in which I dipped a jam jar with a length of string tied around its neck and filled it with peaty water with frog spawn rising to the surface, looking like tapioca – a pudding I have always detested. The bus stopped at the lifeboat houses where Neil, another classmate, got on. Outside Keills school, Innes got on the bus; I found myself wishing that I could get off and remain there for an eighth year – I have always had a desire to wish for something which I know cannot be.

Beyond Keills, the bus entered what was for me less familiar territory as it was beyond the square mile in which I had lived almost every day of my life. I didn't mind the fact that the bus kept stopping at the entrances to farm tracks and small groups of houses as I did not want the bus journey to end. I did not want to reach my destination. But I knew that when the bus went under the bridge at Bridgend and followed the road around Loch Indaal, whose surface rippled in the wind and glowed in brief shafts of sunlight, that the bus would soon enter Bowmore and go up School Brae and park outside the school gates along with buses from Portnahaven and Port Ellen. I was struck by the sheer number of pupils milling noisily around the school gates. I had gone in an instant from less than thirty pupils at Keills to over three hundred at Bowmore.

Those early days at Bowmore were something of a blur. I remember being handed a weekly timetable and I wondered how I would ever be able to follow it. I found the moving from one classroom to another every forty minutes, or eighty minutes, if it was a double period, particularly strange. There were some forty pupils in my class and it seemed peculiar to me that so much time was taken in moving from one room to another, having spent the past four years in the one small room at Keills. I would just about have settled in one classroom when the bell would ring and there would be the clatter of chairs and desks and the rush along the corridor where we would collide with other classes coming out of their rooms and heading to the next one. It all appeared such an unnecessary waste of time to me. I also found it difficult to shift my attention from one subject to the next: to move from English and then to Geography and then to Mathematics and so on seemed bewildering.

I found the teachers a mixed bag and their individuality, or their eccentricity, was reflected in their range of nicknames. There was one female teacher called *The Snipe* due to the length and sharpness of her nose. The shape of her nose reflected the sharpness of her manner. She was one of the few teachers in the school who could control unruly pupils and instilled a necessary element of fear in her class. She taught English but in the fifteen months or so in which I was a pupil at Bowmore, I can't remember anything she taught me. At Keills, I was introduced to certain poems which have stayed with me but *The Snipe* did nothing to add to my verbal treasure trove.

She had a way, like so many teachers, of draining the life and beauty out of a subject, of sucking it dry like a peeled orange left out too long in the sun. In her class, poems were reduced to mental exercises and essays set to answer pointless questions.

Another teacher was referred to as *Hitler* not because he had a small moustache and his wife was called Eva but because in his geography classes he frequently mentioned the Nazi leader. He was a rather arrogant man, although not without a sense of humour, who gave the impression that teaching such a ragbag of pupils was rather beneath him. Still, I later developed a certain fondness for that classroom with its walls papered with maps of countries and continents which I never expected to visit, having only set foot beyond Islay once in my life which turned out to be an experience so traumatic that I had no great desire to repeat it. It was in that classroom I received my first marriage proposal. I remember to this day being passed a note by the pretty, blondish haired girl called Fiona who sat at the desk behind me. I opened the note when *Hitler* had his back turned to the classroom as he wrote on the blackboard a list of the major exports of Brazil or some such fascinating topic. I unfolded the scrap of paper and read the pencilled words: *I want to marry you.* I had heard the rumour that Fiona had taken an inexplicable *fancy* to me but I was rather taken aback by how rapidly her affection for me had progressed, given that I was much too shy to talk to her. Although I did not respond to the note, rather like the *Quality Street* toffee which Valerie gave me a couple of years earlier, I kept this precious note in my pocket long after I had received it and when I was feeling sad and anxious, I would take it out of the inner breast pocket of my blazer and read those five words over again until those pencilled words began to fade just as, I suspect, the passion of the writer would have faded, but much more quickly.

Many decades later, I came across the name of Fiona when browsing through *Friends Reunited.* I was shocked to read that this pretty twelve-year old girl I had remembered so vividly was now a grandmother. I took the courage to message her and remind her that she once asked me to marry her but I did not receive a reply. I can only assume that she did not remember me or the note she wrote and assumed that I was some sort of crank. I felt rather sad that the memory and feelings of receiving that often-read note was entirely in my mind and not in hers, which is so often the case in life.

In the timetable which I carried in my pocket to remind me where I was supposed to be each day, I read that there was to be a double period of *Horticulture Science* which sounded impressive. I had expected to learn something of the botanical nature of my father's job. I was puzzled when the boys in my class were told to line up in a row outside the back door of the school. The girls would attend the equally impressive sounding class of *Domestic Science*. After a long wait, the bald headed headteacher hobbled into view. He had suffered from polio as a child which left him with great difficulty in walking. He was also a somewhat distant man who, like *Hitler*, gave the impression that he would rather be somewhere else – I shared the feeling. He gave us a weak smile and informed us that once the rain had ceased, we would have the privilege of working in his muddy garden. I discovered that the impressive sounding *Horticulture Science* meant weeding the headmaster's garden. One of the most striking features of the garden was that it contained remarkably few plants. If anything had ever actually been planted, it had been destroyed by gales laden with salt spray from Loch Indaal or been eaten by sheep, rabbits or wood pigeons. I wouldn't have minded if this *Horticultural Science* had consisted of planting or seed sowing or pruning or had frames and greenhouses. There were not many weeks when it was dry enough to undertake the mind-expanding task of weeding and on those many weeks when the weather was unsuitable, we would waste the double period and some unfortunate teacher, never the headmaster, would draw the short straw and attempt to keep the unruly behaviour of some twenty boys under control. I can only assume that Domestic Science consisted of washing and drying dishes since the term 'science' was used rather loosely at Bowmore Secondary.

Just as horticulture rarely, if ever, consisted of planting, the navigation class never actually involved sailing. Like the *Horticulture* class, this was a 'boys only' affair which perhaps was just as well as the teacher, *Captain Pugwash* had a rather unhealthy concern with tying knots – I can only speculate what use he made of this skill in his private life. He undertook, certainly in my case, the futile attempt to teach us to tie such complex and bewildering knots as the *half hitch, mooring hitch, icicle hitch* and every other bloody hitch. Not content with demonstrating the *fisherman's knot*, Pugwash considered it vital that his pupils be taught the *double fisherman's knot* – not to be confused with *Fisherman's Friends*. I cannot pretend to remember the names of all the knots that I could never learn to tie but there may have been the *lanyard knot* and *hanson knot*, not to mention the *Japanese square knot* which is presumably subtly different from the *American square dance*. One of the invaluable lessons I took away from my period at Bowmore was that one can never have too many knots in life. Unfortunately, the only knot I ever learned to tie was the reef knot and even that took many attempts. All my attempts at the other knots with exotic names ended up with me unintentionally handcuffing myself. I shall always remember the long suffering and pitying looks which *Captain Pugwash* gave me as he would to any other pupil he regarded as an imbecile. He was, after all, a kind and decent man despite his unfortunate fetish for tying knots.

Along with the dreaded knots, he attempted to teach us how to read navigation charts, but again, I was hampered by my inability to hold the chart the right way up. After a year or so of quite literally tying myself in knots and running aground on sea charts, there was one morning when the *Captain* who had long since lost his imaginary ship, led us down the brae to the harbour. With sunlight caressing the surface of Loch Indaal, I thought that at long last we would be taken out on a boat and I would for the first time in my life, sail around the sea loch. Of course, I should have known better and all we did when we got to the pier was to stand and listen to *Pugwash* drone on. If I had paid any attention to what he said, I might have remembered a little of it. All I remember is walking back up the brae with that nagging thought of what might have been if we had actually set sail. In retrospect, I can only assume that the *Captain*, like my mother, suffered from sea sickness. If only I had known at the time, I could have suggested that he place his large bottom on a sheet of newspaper, a broadsheet, but only if it wasn't too shiny. During this period when the boys were navigating without boats, I assume that the girls were sewing with imaginary needles and thread. Nothing at Bowmore could be taken at face value which is one of the few valuable lessons I learned during my time there.

Another of the characterful teachers at the school was the bow-legged art teacher who walked as if he had spent many years riding the plains and cattle ranching in my favourite television western: *Laramie*. Just as the *Captain* had lost his ship, he had lost his horse. He wore colourful tight jeans and boots which only served to emphasize the curvature of his legs. I can't remember anything he said about art but I do remember his tale of how one day, he came across a rabbit who was suffering from myxomatosis and how with the large sheath knife he happened to have on him at the time, he slit the throat of the creature to put it out of his misery. Although this was no doubt a compassionate act under the circumstances, the image of this cowboy wandering around the island with a large knife lodged in my mind. There was also a certain boastfulness about the way in which he recounted this tale which I found distasteful. Another of his boasts was informing us that he never rolled up his strap, his *Lochgelly*, as other teachers did, so that it kept its rigidity and hurt all the more. He opened his desk, took out the strap and held it up to the class like a prize exhibit to reveal how stiff and unbending it was. It was as if he kept it in his desk like a snake which he fed with the occasional small rodent to keep its strength up. Admittedly, he very rarely used it to belt a pupil but there was one morning when he did use it and it was across the hand of a pale faced boy from Port Ellen who never looked well, as if he suffered from some undiagnosed condition. I saw the fear in the boys' eyes as he was ordered to come out in front of the room to receive his punishment from messing around with paint. I heard the two sharp cracks like small explosions. The boy shuffled his way back to his desk and then he began to sob uncontrollably, holding his burning right hand in his left. The incident reminded me of the belting of Sandy in Keills and I experienced the same burning sense of injustice. In school, as in the world outside, it is so often the weak who suffer the most and who suffer with a bewildered look in their eyes.

The classes I detested most were woodwork and metalwork. They were my first two periods on a Monday morning and I began to dread going back to school after each weekend. The teacher was a bald, bespectacled, sharp faced, bad tempered little man who was filled with a sense of his own remarkable abilities. Like so many classes in Bowmore, a great deal of time was spent on achieving very little. In the woodwork room, you always had to wait your turn to use some tool or other and hours past with nothing to show for it. On looking back, the only achievement I can recall throughout my first year of woodwork was making a letter rack and even then, I had glued the back of mine the wrong way round and it had also an unfortunate, lopsided appearance. Although I took it home, it was never used, presumably because my mother was too embarrassed by my efforts to display it. The teacher understandably shared the same opinion of my intellectual abilities, or lack of them, as the *Captain*, but instead of his kind, pitying look, all I received for my efforts was a contemptuous sneer. Unlike the biscuit barrel which my mother so proudly won at a whist drive on one never to be forgotten winter evening in the dilapidated Ballygrant Hall, my letter rack was never given pride of place on the dresser but kept decently out of sight. If I should ever come across this much maligned item, it would bring back the shy, nervous twelve-year old with all his inner doubts and longings almost more than any other object. However, I don't expect the one creation of my woodwork days at Bowmore ever to resurface as I suspect that my father may have used it to light the fire in the range when he was short of kindlers one morning.

One of the most curious aspects of many in the school was that every Friday afternoon, all the pupils, with the exception of those deemed to be the most academic who studied Latin, were 'treated' to a two-hour film show. Unfortunately, the film show consisted almost entirely of racing car rallies. For a seemingly interminable two hours, we were led into a darkened room to test the limits of our boredom. Those rallies seemed to invariably take place along snow-laden tracks in forests somewhere in Finland or Norway and the drivers would have unpronounceable names which the commentator would repeat with rising excitement as if the result was a matter of life or death. It was always something of a mystery to me how anyone could derive any excitement from such a pointless exercise. It's strange but no one appeared to question why we were subjected, through no fault of our own, to watching car rallies on a large, flickering screen every Friday afternoon. It was only later that I was informed that the school was sent those reels for free and the headteacher presumably thought that the school might as well show them, if only to keep the pupils amused and quiet. If that was the reason, it failed on both counts. After some twenty minutes, the pupils would become more and more restless and rowdy. It was usually the task of the gym teacher to keep the pupils in order, but after an hour of the roar of revved up cars and the snow which refused to stop falling, his task became almost impossible. So little attention did I pay that I wasn't entirely sure if those film reels consisted of a series of different car rallies or it was the same one which went on without end where the chequered flag, if there was one, was never actually lowered. Perhaps somewhere still, that car rally is still going on and the snow is still falling silently on the tall spruces and all those numbered cars are going round and round a forest where the end is beyond everyone's reach.

Nicknames at the school were not always given fairly. There was one relatively elderly lady teacher who was called *The Witch* for reasons I was never able to fathom as she came across as a rather kind person with a sweet, humorous smile. She did have a propensity for handing out lines which consisted not of the hundred or more repetitions of a single line but the copying of an article from a newspaper. The writing of lines was surely more civilized than striking a pupil's hand with a leather belt.

Another elderly – in the eyes of children – female teacher who impressed me by her kindness was nicknamed *The Pheasant*. Again, I had no idea how she came by this nickname and I didn't like to ask and reveal my ignorance. Perhaps it was because she wore a feather in her hat. She was the most impressive of all the teachers I had at Bowmore. She taught music and her room was at the furthest end of the corridor from the main entrance. To enter that music room was to be transported to a different world. Even her classroom had a different appearance to the other classrooms. There was panelling on the walls and ceiling, perhaps to enhance the acoustics. *The Pheasant* had a way of controlling a class without the use of handing out lines and certainly never reduced to using the strap. She appeared to be able to control the class simply by holding the attention of the pupils, even those who on the surface had little musical ability.

There was a large piano in the room and *The Pheasant* would play brief tunes on it and the sounds of the notes had a mellow timbre which echoed within the walls. She succeeded in teaching even the less able pupils to write a few notes of music on a sheet of music paper with its rows of five lines. She would patiently teach us how to draw a treble clef and I found pleasure in making the curves with my pencil. We would sing and even those, such as myself, with no voice for singing would take pleasure in joining in without the fear of being mocked by their inability to hold a tune. She had a record player and introduced us to the thrill of orchestral music which would resound within those panelled walls. Like most of the class, I had never heard a full orchestra before. Through my father's wireless, I rarely heard music of any kind, it was almost always speech of one kind or another. Only occasionally would I hear a song by Jim Reeves in a magazine programme and my father would sing along, as best he could, to *I won't forget you* or *I love you because*. Sometimes, there might be a Scottish folk song sung by Kathleen Ferrier such as *The Keel Row*, or perhaps a rendition of *Danny Boy* and my father would join in with *the pipes, the pipes are calling* and then give up. On television, I would hear only the songs and accordion music of *The White Heather Club* or the Gaelic songs on 'Se Ur Beatha and later, *Top of the Pops*. On my sisters' transistor, there was only pop music to be heard and on our record player, there would also mostly be pop music played and of course, songs such as *The Waters of Kylesku*. Radio 3, if we could have received it, may only have been an inch or so further along on the dial but it may as well have been a mile.

The first orchestral piece which I heard in that room was Eric Coates' *The Dam Busters March* and I could sense the collective power of the instruments which sounded like the surge of waves against the rocks around the Wee Pier, but I loved the gentler music still more. *The Pheasant* would also play us extracts from Saint Saens *Carnival of Animals* and I found myself moved by the sweet sadness of *The Swan* which, in my mind, would be gliding across the far side of Loch Allan on those stilled days of autumn when its surface held a mirror to the sky and the leaves of the rowans were almost motionless around the bays. She would play us extracts from Beethoven's *Pastoral Symphony* and point to where the clarinets made the call of the cuckoo, a sound which formed the background notes to my island summers.

In that music room, time seemed to stall and yet, at the same time, move so quickly. Whereas the double period of woodwork or technical drawing or navigation seemed to last an eternity, the double period of music would often end too soon and the sound of the bell would break through my trance. The ideal teacher is one who instils in the pupil a thirst to explore a subject further and deeper and *The Pheasant* was just such a teacher. With her modesty and unassuming manner, I expect she would not have been aware of the lasting gift she imparted to all those pupils throughout her many years at Bowmore.

There were two other teachers I admired who were spared the indignity of having an unflattering nickname bestowed upon them. One was a young lady with a gentle, sensitive manner – qualities which can be something of a disadvantage when dealing with teenagers – called Miss Love. Perhaps her strength lay in her seeming vulnerability in that pupils felt the need to protect her. I know that I did.

The other teacher was a young, blonde-haired lady who taught Gaelic. I still vividly remember the day when she was given the news that her mother had died and I caught a glimpse of her in the classroom in floods of tears. I believe that she died young but she, like so many people in my past, retain a shadowy existence in my memory and, from time to time, flare into life like the blown embers of a dying fire.

Apart from the music lessons, what I enjoyed most of all were the games of football we played at lunchtime. The tarred back playground would be crowded with boys – no girl played – and the sides would rarely, if ever, be evenly numbered but that in some respects added to the enjoyment. I was still an infant when my father took myself and George to the back lawn which was just outside the potting shed where the grass was thick and long. As it was not seen from the Big House, it did not need to be mowed and rolled like a bowling green. There was a hedge which ran along one side of this long back lawn which my father would spend an entire day clipping with his hand shears. When I got older, I would help him in this twice-yearly task. In July, the midges would rise from the small, damp leaves and I would pause frequently to scratch the itch in my hair, neck, and bare arms. It was on this length of coarse grass that I first remember being taught how to kick a ball and to control it when it was passed to me. Despite my father's best efforts to persuade him to kick the ball with his right foot, George would persist in kicking with his left.

I enjoyed playing football at Keills but my pleasure was limited by the small number of boys who played the game. At Bowmore, there was certainly no shortage of boys and the sheer number of players I had to beat made the pleasure of scoring a goal all the sweeter. It was only through playing football that I felt at one with the other boys in the school. Goal posts at one end consisted of the shelter and at the other end, there were two lines marked on the boundary wall with chalk. It was in this shelter that we would so often wait impatiently for the rain to cease or a shower to pass over so that we could return to our game.

CHAPTER 29

Daphne Oxenford and Lucozade

It was when playing football on that tarmac playground on my first, and what turned out to be my last winter at Bowmore, that I seriously injured my right ankle which would lead to weeks of pain and six or seven weeks largely spent in bed. It was only when I tried to get out of bed the next morning after what seemed a minor injury at the time, that I realized that I was unable to walk. When I placed my right foot on the ground, I experienced waves of pain. I found that I simply could not get down the stairs on my own. In my seven years at Keills, I had rarely missed a day but I realized that I would have no choice but to stay at home. After three days or so, my father called the doctor – in the days when a GP would undertake home visits. This doctor whose nickname was Dr Joe was not known for his gentle manner and he showed little tenderness when he moved my ankle from side to side to check to see if it was broken. He came to the conclusion that it was not, but that he would arrange for an X-ray at the small cottage hospital in Bowmore. Since my parents had no transport, a few days later an ambulance came to collect me and take me to the hospital. As I was helped down the stairs and lifted into the ambulance, I found myself anxiously wondering if I would ever walk again since the week or so in bed had done nothing to help my ankle or to stop the constant, throbbing pain. It felt strange to be driven along the road to school with the landscape shadowed as I looked through the darkened windows of the ambulance, knowing that school was not my destination. I had been to this hospital a few years earlier when my brother accidentally pushed me against the wall of the disused outdoor toilet at Keills when we were playing a game. My head hit the wall and it began to bleed and I was driven by taxi to the hospital. I remembered on the way home, with a bandage over my head, being allowed to help steer the car by the kind driver as we drove a little way along past Loch Indaal. As the ambulance reached Bowmore around lunchtime, I thought of the game of football in the playground which would be continuing without me. I can remember little of the process involved in having my first ever X-ray but the result was that my ankle was not broken – always assuming that the probably outdated X-ray machine was in full working order – which made my inability to walk even more inexplicable. I was sent off with tablets to ease the constant pain and told to rest in bed for an indefinite period of time.

Week after week, I lay in bed in that box room bedroom watching the brief hours of daylight filter through the thin curtains each morning and fade as dusk slowly descended in the winter afternoons. Some mornings, I would be awakened by the pattering of rain drops blown against the glass. On other mornings, sunlight would stream through and form patterns across the shiny linoleum floor and the worn rug by the side of the bed. I would hear sounds from the kitchen below as my father scraped the ashes from the grate and put the pot of porridge on the range. Some mornings, if I was not still in the land of often disturbing dreams, I would hear George get up and hear his footsteps on the stairs and then echo over the linoleum in the hall as he made his way into the chilly bathroom.

My days would have seemed like an eternal present if it wasn't punctuated by the arrival of meals usually brought by my father: breakfast, invariably of porridge then the cup of tea and two tea biscuits, around 10.00am, buttered together the wrong side up; lunch, which we called dinner, was the main meal of the day, consisting often of my mother's home-made soup which was her speciality; scotch broth, lentil or tatty soup, followed by her rice pudding or custard; then instant coffee and perhaps a chocolate digestive biscuit, if money allowed, around 3.00pm. Tea would be around 5.30pm which in the winter months would sometimes be another bowl of porridge, and perhaps a cup of tea and another biscuit for supper. My mother tended to cook the same main meal on the same day of each week but sometimes our diet varied a little if the gamekeeper brought a brace of pheasants or grouse or a hunk of venison and sometimes brown trout which were always fried in oatmeal. If we were unlucky, he would only bring a rabbit which was not at all popular with any member of the family, partly because of its taste and partly because being reduced to eating rabbit was for my mother, in particular, a sign of shameful poverty. I always knew by the day what treat or otherwise was in store. We were of course fortunate in having the fruit and vegetables from the walled garden which helped to supplement the family income and to enhance our diet. More welcome even than the meals were the painkillers which my father would hand to me every four hours or so which I would wash down with a glass of tepid *Lucozade*. The textured bottle with its golden wrapper which rustled when you touched it stood on the bedside table next to me and I would reach for it from time to time and feel its sticky sides. Whenever a bottle of *Lucozade* was on display, it was a sign that one of the family was ill and in need of a pick-me-up.

My only amusement to help pass the long hours of each day was the transistor radio which stood beside the *Lucozade* bottle on the bedside table. There were a few books handed down through the generations in the house but I was not an avid reader as a child. I was responsive to the few poems I had been introduced to at Keills but it would never have occurred to my parents to ever buy or borrow a poetry book. My radio was my constant companion during those weeks in bed. I would begin by listening to the morning service on the BBC Home station. I liked some of the hymns, a few of which we sang at school, such as *O Jesus I Have Promised, There Is a Green Hill Far Away* and *The Day Thou Gavest Lord Has Ended*. The solemn strains of the latter two hymns had a particular appeal to me. I would listen to some of the other programmes on the Home Service in the mornings. Even though it was intended for infants, I think the programme which gave me the most pleasure was *Listen with Mother* which was presented by Daphne Oxenford with the daily repetition of the sentences: *Are you sitting comfortably? Then I'll begin*, spoken in a posh BBC voice, appealed to me partly for its silliness. The story inevitably beginning with *Once upon a time* – a time which never was – with its often, trite moral message was both laughable and comforting. Rather like the Enid Blyton novels I read, the programme conjured up in my mind a cosy world far removed from mine in which the Mummy and

Daddy were always thoughtful and kind, never made tired or angry with exhausting work, or had the constant anxiety of how to pay bills; who never spoke bitterly to each other with accusations which they came to regret but the hurt they caused lingered. Although the well-spoken children in those stories were sometimes naughty, they were free of the conflicts and jealousies and deep longings that I had for something different.

The part of *Listen with Mother* I loved most and which was my main reason for listening to it was the tune which was played at the end of each episode. The slow notes of the piano which sounded in that small box room seemed to echo the longings which I felt. Not just the longing to walk again but those indefinable longings for something other than the life I led. Even through the static, those piano notes had a clarity and a space between them which allowed me to dream. It was only much later that I learnt that that piece of music with all its beauty and autumnal sadness was by the French composer Gabriel Faure and entitled *Berceuse* which was part of his *Dolly Suite*. That is the piece of music which evokes my weeks in bed more than any other. Of course, I did not know that it would be weeks before I could walk, and walk without pain again, I felt that I was serving a sentence with no release date.

After my escape with Daphne Oxenford, I would turn the dial to the Light Programme which was transmitted on Long Wave where the reception was better. I would listen to pop music and drift in and out of sleep brought on by the painkilling tablets. A song which was often played in those afternoons was Donovan's *Mellow Yellow* which seemed to fit those times when awakening merged with dreams as the raindrops blown by a gust would sound against the window as if they were knocking to get in. As the winter afternoons drew on with their watered sunlight, I would watch the shadows lengthen along the linoleum and form different patterns. I felt a comfort in the return of dusk each day as I knew that the school day would have ended and I felt less out of things. It was not that I missed school as such, it's just that I felt so cut off from the world. I did however miss those lunchtime games of football and longed to be able to take part in them again.

Because each day merged so seamlessly into another with no variation, it was as if time stood still to match my immobility. The words of a poem I had learnt at Keills kept coming back to me. It was by Robert Louis Stevenson and was called *The Land of Counterpane*. The poem describes how a sick child who is confined to bed imagines himself in charge of a great army and navy and how he built cities in the folds of his bed clothes. I could not relate to such feats of imagination but I could partly relate to the last verse in the sense of stillness. However, my own land of counterpane was not always pleasant.

> *I was the giant great and still*
> *That sits upon the pillow-hill*
> *And sees before him, dale and plain*
> *The pleasant land of counterpane.*

After weeks of rest, I found that the pain in my ankle lessened and I did not need the four hourly painkillers. I would ease myself out from below the layers of blankets and by holding on to the iron headboard, struggle to get to my feet and at last be able to stand without anyone's help. I would look out of the small window and see once more the familiar world from which I had been removed. There was the yard across the drive; the bare leafed apple trees espaliered on the whitewashed wall which had been darkened with weeks of rain; the red coal shed door. There were the fuchsia bushes under which the hens sheltered in summer showers. From the layers of trees above the yard, I heard a power saw which meant that the forestry workers were cutting some fallen branches or taking down a diseased tree. In the spaces between the screams of the saw, I heard the distant sound of waves which I had not heard for so long as the box room was at the front of the house facing away from the sea.

From then on, I was able to go downstairs, leaning on my father's arm, in the evening to watch television and see Percy Thrower hang up his jacket on a nail as he entered his greenhouse and see men in kilts and women with tartan sashes dance reels in the *White Heather Club* – on the black and white screen – mostly white in our case – you had to imagine the varying colours of tartan. Once more, I saw the ranchers of *Laramie* with their herds of cattle raising dust and *Perry Mason* win another case with the guilty party confessing all, just in time to spare the innocent from a lifetime in prison or the electric chair. I felt a certain comfort in finding it was all as I had left it.

On my first steps out of the house, I found that the air was softened by the whispered promises of spring. The leaf buds were swelling on the sycamore tree which stood at the side of our house whose lower branches I so often sat on and looked down on the world. The sea sounded differently, each wave like a lingering sigh. I heard the birds singing loudly and more urgently as if they were aware that there was much to do. On the triangle of lawn below our front porch, I saw the heads of daisies elbowing their way above the level of the grass. As I carefully walked up the drive to the garden, on the bank, the pink, powdery tassels of flowering currants were nodding in the breeze as if in agreement with each other, spreading their perfume and blending it with the coconut scents of gorse. On the bank beneath Granny Chisholm's old house, sun strands made the daffodils glow a deeper yellow, their leaves glistening with raindrops of recent showers.

I opened the garden door and felt the warmth of the sheltered breeze against my face as if I had entered a gentler world. I felt that if I stood still and listened closely enough, I would hear the surge of spring growth. The last time I had seen the gooseberries and the blackcurrant bushes, their stems were bare as if they revealed the skeletons of themselves but now, they were clothed in small, half-unfurled leaves of a delicate green. Along the trellis, sweet pea plants were just beginning to reach up with their tendrils, clinging on to eventually climb higher and higher, reaching up to the light. I walked up the steps which led to the square of paving slabs which separated the two greenhouses. In the middle border, roses displayed their shiny, dark green leaves. In summer, with an ancient putter and a nectarine stone for a ball, those paving slabs provided hours of entertainment as we tried to putt around the square without the stone landing on the cracks between each slab. The wrinkled shape of the nectarine stone added to the difficulty of the task.

The door of the bottom greenhouse was open and I limped my way down the steps and caught those familiar mixed scents of geraniums, putty, linseed oil and the lingering fumes of pink paraffin. To enter that greenhouse was to bathe oneself in scents. I then made my way up the steps and into the top greenhouse in which the espaliered nectarines grew. Soon, the blowsy, pinkish blossom would appear again along the spread-eagled stems and my father would once more conduct an unseen orchestra with his baton, wrapped around with a rabbit's tail. To be a gardener is to bind yourself to the cycle of the seasons and be moved around and around with them. Then at the hour of your death, your body merges into the soil you have so long worked to become one with the circular motions of the earth.

Gradually, each day I found that I was able to walk without pain and without a limp. Although I had felt isolated at times spending much time on my own in that box bedroom, I came to rather like the routine I had created for myself. I especially liked that drowsy sensation of drifting in and out of dream. Still, it felt wonderful to be able to walk with ease. I was also able to do what I doubted I would ever be able to do again and that was to kick a football. I knew that it would be sometime before I would be able to run around in the yard with a ball at my feet, hearing the imaginary roar of the crowd and see myself as Willie Henderson racing down the right wing at Ibrox Park. The one drawback to being able to walk again was that I would have to return to Bowmore Secondary, a prospect which I found almost as daunting as it had been when I stepped into that school for the first time last August. I felt as if I would have to begin all over again and adapt to the ringing of the bell and the traipsing along the corridor to one classroom after another. Most depressing of all was the prospect of the woodwork classes with the instructions I could not follow; the navigation class with its bewildering maps and knots; the technical drawing with its three-dimensional shapes which may as well have been four dimensional for all I understood of it.

Despite my attempt to hold back the clock, the Monday morning of my return to school came around and I found myself walking down the drive with George who was in the enviable position of his last year at Bowmore. I watched the bus go down to the pier to turn and then come up the brae and stop outside Gate Lodge. As I stepped on board the bus, I felt the eyes of the pupils on me as if I had made an unexpected return from the dead. I gazed out of the bus window at the familiar landscape and houses and the familiar faces of pupils who had been travelling this route in all those weeks without me. The bus reached the car park outside the school and I entered the melee.

Even more than on the first day, I was struck by the sheer noise after my weeks of near silence broken by the gentle voice of Daphne Oxenford asking me personally if I was sitting comfortably. In the noise, I tried to return in my mind to the gentle, spaced notes of Faure's *Berceuse*. Still, I felt comforted by the questions as to how I was by some of my classmates and by those who had not spoken to me before. They seemed, to my surprise, pleased to see me return as did some of my teachers. Even the sharp faced woodwork teacher was almost pleasant to me as I walked into his room with the smell of wood shavings and varnish which I had come to detest. I fondly imagined that the next time I shaved too much off a piece of wood or stuck it the wrong way round, I would be treated with more consideration but I was wrong on that account. Lunchtime came around and after the meal, I joined in the football and found that the other boys tackled me more gently when I had the ball which made a pleasant change from being kicked. Apart from the football, I enjoyed most stepping once again into the wood panelled room of *The Pheasant* who greeted me with her sweet, rather other-worldly smile. That room reminded me a little of my own bedroom in which time moved differently.

My first year at Bowmore passed and the long summer holidays came around again. It wasn't long into the beginning of my second year at the school that my life was to change and nothing would ever be quite the same again.

CHAPTER 30

Mainland Dreams

Even after thirteen years or so, my mother still could not adapt to island life and she nagged constantly at my father to look for another job on the mainland where she fondly imagined she would find an escape from her prison whose insurmountable walls were the sea. The other powerful influence on my father was his elder brother Alex, who had never left his childhood place of Kilmacolm. Every few weeks my father, usually on a Sunday evening with the glowing lumps of coal shifting restlessly in the grate, took out his blue lined writing pad from the drawer and filled page after page with his barely decipherable scrawl, rather like a hen scratching in the dust, filled with memories of the sunlit childhood he shared with his brother when they were poor but supposedly happy. There were memories of their time wandering along the golf course in search of lost golf balls which they would sell for a few precious pennies as if those golf balls symbolized their lost childhood. There were the paper rounds which would take them out to Bridge of Weir with its Quarriers Homes in which orphaned children were housed. There were the shared memories of the rare treat of the *poky hat* from the *Tallys* and the *poky hat of chips* with its odour of vinegar and the steam rising in the chilled evening air – theirs was a childhood of *poky hats*. There was the excitement of getting a bus to Ibrox Park to watch their Rangers' heroes, being given a *carry over* the turnstile as they could not afford to pay for a ticket. My father's face would take on a dream-like expression as his pen moved across the flimsy paper with a scraping sound. When he had finished, he stuffed the pages into a small envelope and stuck on a skewed stamp. A couple of weeks later, *Donnie the Post* would park his van below our house and wait until myself or my brother would run to collect the letters or parcels and there would be an envelope with my uncle's familiar handwriting. His letters would imply that they could relive those past times more fully if only they did not live so far apart, not realizing that it is often through writing that the past can come more fully alive.

My father searched the *Situations Vacant* columns of the *Gardeners' Chronicle* and *The Oban Times*, egged on by my mother. Without the influences of his wife and brother, he may have been content to remain on Islay, particularly given his natural inclination for prevarication. However, although he had lived nearly all his adult life in the countryside, often in remote places, he was not a country lover but a small-town person at heart. It was only his job and the house which went along with it that led him to the Highlands and the Islands where large private estates were still quite prevalent after the Second World War. His job applications led him to attend an interview for a gardening job on an estate near Appin, not all that far from where he had previously worked at Melfort. He was offered the position but for some reason he rejected it. It may well have been that it was too far from his brother in Kilmacolm and his fondly remembered childhood there.

When I began my second year at Bowmore, I was conscious of the fact that I may well not be at the school before the year had ended. My premonition proved to be well founded as I was not even allowed to complete the first term. My father had come across a gardening job at Sorn Castle in Ayrshire and he sent off his application and was offered an interview. Although he had no connection with Ayrshire, his brother made much of the fact that Sorn was only an hour's drive from Kilmacolm. Unlike my father, Uncle Alex was the proud possessor of a car. My father was gone for two days and he came back keen to accept the job he had been offered. Before accepting the position, he wanted my mother to travel to Ayrshire in order to view the Gate Lodge which would be her new home. She took the courage to board the ferry and undertake the sea crossing she so much dreaded. I think that it was only the possibility of a final escape from the island which impelled her to set sail again, no doubt clutching a newspaper for the voyage – my mother rarely, if ever, read a newspaper, for her it was simply something to sit on or to stuff inside wet wellingtons or shoes to dry them on the hearth. Having seen the house in Ayrshire, she came back with reservations about the dampness of the lodge but her desire to leave Islay was so compelling that she overlooked this fact which was later to aggravate her bronchitis and her lumbago for the remaining years of her life.

Another compelling reason for her to agree to the move to Sorn was that there was a twice weekly bus to the large town of Kilmarnock which passed the lodge gates and the prospect of a regular bus trip to a place with an infinitely wider range of shops than Bowmore was irresistible. She loved to sit on a bus and gaze out on the passing scenes. Rather like a fractious child, her mood was soothed by the act of motion. Of course, given my mother's unfortunate lack of a sense of direction, when she got to Kilmarnock, she frequently got lost. It was the large stores such as *Woolworths* which confused her the most with doors which exited on to different streets which was never a problem in Port Ellen or Bowmore. Sadly, it was not long after we moved to Sorn that the bus service to Kilmarnock was discontinued, leaving my mother, in some respects, even more marooned than she had felt on Islay.

Not knowing, perhaps mercifully, what the future had in store, it was decided that we would leave Islay – I say *we* but I don't recall anyone asking me if I wanted to leave. When I told my classmates at school that I was soon to leave the island, they expressed their envy of me being able to ride the roller coasters and other fairground attractions in the holiday coastal town of Ayr which they had heard about, although I hadn't. I never did ride that roller coaster of their dreams. I was promised, or threatened, with a send-off on my last day at school. However, I did not return to school on the week before we left and my father posted back my text books. Memories of my short time at Bowmore remain with me and the ghosts of familiar faces flit through my mind from time to time. However, the school and its pupils do not loom nearly as large in my memory as my time at Keills and those hours spent gazing out of the wide windows of the Wee Room and the Big Room at the wind-blown grass and the interrogating crows balancing on the stone wall and the chalk dust drifting down from the blackboard on those afternoons in which time could not be measured by the hands of any clock.

Although I felt a small sense of excitement at moving to another place, more than anything, I felt a deep sense of losing something which I felt I would never be able to recover. In the week of our leaving, I walked around the small world which I had inhabited for the thirteen and a half years of my life as if trying to gather precious fragments which I could take with me. Everywhere I went, I sensed that it would be for the last time. I walked up the drive past the garden and around by Granny Chisholm's house, now lying empty and echoing only with voices of the past. I learned later that when my father informed the factor that he was leaving, he had been offered this house to live in while much needed repairs to our own house were carried out. My father refused it, no doubt persuaded to do so by his wife and brother. To live in that house above the garden would have felt like a strange homecoming to me as I so vividly remembered those afternoons that I had spent in that living room with its small window which let in so little light that even in summer, it contained the gloom of winter. I heard in my mind the languid voice of the old woman as it rose and fell as she recounted days which had gone. There was the slow hissing of the wet coal in the stubborn fire in the grate and the West Highland terrier, who looked as ancient as its owner, slumped on the rug, its body twitching as it dreamed or awoke from a dream. There was the loud ticking of the grandfather clock which sounded more loudly still when the conversation lulled.

Just below the house, there was the path which led through the woods which I had walked so many times before, my footsteps leaving indentations on the wet, spongy moss. I knew that each indentation would soon fade and the path would appear as if I had never stepped along it. In a gap between the trees with the tinged, falling leaves of November, I could see the bluish grey sliver of the Sound and the bare brown hills of Jura on the other side, looking as impassive as always. Instead of following the path which led to the gate which opened to the moor, I took the branching path which passed below our house. I passed the hollow stems of the plant whose name I never knew and which I used to hack down, pretending that I was macheting my way through a jungle. I walked further along the path to where the sea could be seen more clearly through a gap in the trees. The clouds dispersed and the mist which so often shrouded the rounded peaks of the Paps of Jura lifted and they were caressed by fingers of sunlight. I stood on the white bridge and looked down the stone steps which led to the Wee Pier and to the arch of overhanging rock where the body of the killed sheep had long since merged with the sparse soil. I walked along Lover's Lane, which had long since lost its lovers, where, each spring, the perfumes of gorse, azaleas and salt breezes blended to create a scent which no one could ever distil. The sea shimmered below me and only the cries of sea birds dispersed the silence. I went up the steps at the side of the Big House and I stood on the balcony at the side of the front lawn where the flagpole jutted out. The flag was down as Mr Schroder was not in residence. I gazed all the way up the Sound and I could see all the way along the east coast of Islay where no road could reach and I could see the coast of Colonsay, an island I had never visited, and the faint outline of the mountains of Mull in the now piercing clarity of the autumn air. The awareness that I was soon to leave this place intensified its beauty.

I walked across the lawn whose mown stripes of summer had faded and, down the drive, I stood beside the tree which had been our lookout post from which to view the world below. Port, as it so often was, on the days when there was no ferry and the shop was closed for half-day, giving Lizzie, the woman who served in the shop a well-earned rest, was deserted. There was no cargo ship to take cattle to the mainland markets with the barking of dogs and the shouts of men waving sticks. There was just Peter, one of the brothers who operated the small passenger ferry to Jura, slowly walking down the steps of his brother's house, across from the shop, and making his way along the pier to his small cottage in Freeport where the wake of the ferry as it left the pier shoved the pebbles up the gentle slope of the bay. I remembered that he once took me with him on his crossing to Jura, and I at last set foot on the island that I had gazed upon year after year for the first and only time. As he walked, he was carefully holding something in his hand, probably an egg for his tea, given to him by his brother's wife, which I had seen him carry before when I was on the pier. He was a shy, gentle man who never married. That delicately held egg seemed to symbolize a gentle and fragile way of life I was so soon to leave behind.

I looked down on the hotel bar which was not yet open and at the whitewashed wall where I would never again sit on stilled evenings of summer expectantly waiting with my brother for my father to bring us *Golden Wonder* crisps and a stone-coloured bottle of ginger beer. As I stood below the tree, a few of the falling leaves landed gently on my head and I knew that they would go on falling after I had gone. The autumn winds would make them form drifts along the edges of the drive and they would deepen and deepen and would lie there until someone else came to burn them with the sulphur scent of struck matches and the pages of the newspapers opening to reveal their dated headlines. The ashes of the rows of fires would glow a deeper red as dusk descended.

I retraced my footsteps back up the drive but instead of going past the Big House, I took the turning to the right which led up around the back of the garden, past the rhododendrons where I once had my hide from which to look out on the world unseen. Further up the slope of the drive, there were some fallen chestnuts with their spiky cases crushed by a *Land Rover* or tractor before they could be gathered. I wondered if in the autumns to come, anyone would gather the chestnuts as my brother and I had done for as long as I could remember. I stood for a while and watched the chestnut leaves with their curled palms, broad fingers and thick veins, falling slowly through the moist air. I walked along the path behind the garden wall on which the mud seldom dried out. I felt that my footsteps would last a little longer there before the mud closed over them. I stood leaning on the wall and looked down on the garden. The row of blackcurrants along the wall were losing their yellowed leaves. The left dahlias with their heavy heads were blackening; the sweet peas had formed their seed pods; only a few rose blooms remained, but not for much longer. The grape vine against the wall between the greenhouses was revealing its bare stems, like a skeleton beneath the flesh. The panes of the greenhouses mirrored the strands of autumn sunlight like the motionless surface of the Lily Loch, above which a red deer stood watching and waiting.

Chapter 31

Voices within Walls

My last full day on Islay came around. I can remember little of the details of the packing and the coming of the removal van. It was as if I was a part of something unreal, following paths where some unsettling dream led me. I do remember the shock of seeing the empty kitchen which was the centre of our house. It looked so much smaller than I had imagined with the table and chairs gone and the horsehair sofa at the side of the range removed. As I walked across the room, I heard my footsteps echo on the faded patterns of linoleum as if they were not my own. It was the first morning I can ever remember when the fire in the grate was not lit: that doused fire seemed to symbolize a life which had come to an end. That fire would no doubt be lit again by others but not by us. In my mind, future dwellers in that house would be regarded as mere squatters with no real right to be there.

I walked through the kitchen door to the hall where the Christmas tree stood each year, with its precariously balanced angel and its lights casting moving shadows across the ceiling. The carpet in the front room in which we sat for only two weeks in the year had been lifted and my footsteps went on echoing across bare floorboards. The door of the cupboard which had been so often locked as it contained my mother's precious handbag – that handbag which she had watched floating away from her in the flooded ferry as death drew near on my one holiday – was strangely open. I walked up the stairs and into the box room which had been my bedroom all my life to find that it had itself been reduced to an empty box. The room which earlier in the year had become my world as I lay there unable to get out of it without help, often in a state between dream and awakening, watching dusk come around each slow afternoon, immersed in a land of my own imagining.

I then entered my parents' bedroom next door, the room in which I had been born very early one May morning, before dawn cast its purplish light across the Sound below and revealed the Paps, brooding and watching like an impassive, all-seeing mother. Of course, I remember nothing of that day but I like to think that the sun broke through the clouds later and lit up the waves of bluebells in the Dunlossit woods and their honeyed scent was blended in breezes with the scent of primroses on the mossed banks and with the coconut perfumes of gorse on the path from the Lily Loch. Imagining the world before, and just after you were born, is like imagining the world after you have died. I know that my mother was ill and stayed in bed for weeks after I was born and she was bound to feel that the price of my birth was much too high. I walked next into my sisters' bedroom and remembered all those Sunday evenings which echoed to Radio Luxemburg, the pop songs rising and falling on waves of interference. That sense of distance enhanced the music, lending it an air of romance. It was the closest I came to the feel of the so-called *swinging sixties* in my secluded childhood. I walked back down the uncarpeted stairs. The house was so full of echoes. I sensed that the walls contained our voices but could be heard only by those who knew how to listen to them. When I was angry and felt a deep sense of injustice as an infant, I would imagine that I could summon creatures who lived within those walls to come out and wreak vengeance on those who had upset me. Where were those avenging angels now when I most needed them?

We were to spend our last night on Islay in the *Big House* as all the furniture, even those pieces riddled with woodworm, had been removed, like our lives, from our house. Apart from that one evening of entertainment when we were invited to sit on the stairs and look down on our social superiors who sat on comfortable chairs below us, I had not been further into the *Big House* than the pantry with its cool, marble tiled floor with its window covered with mesh where my father left the fruit, flowers and vegetables. Now I was to have the privilege of entering a bedroom – not one of the best ones of course – and sleep on a bed with a tall, brass headboard.

In the off-season, there was only the housekeeper, Marion, who stayed in the house. She was an elegant, middle-aged lady who my nephew, Brian, said looked like the Queen. She never seemed to have a hair out of place, her face skilfully and discreetly applied with makeup, she looked more aristocratic than many who came as guests to the house. In the middle of winter, I would see only a single light in all the many windows of the Big House and that light would be from the housekeeper's parlour. That small window which cast an oblong of light on the lawn looked like a small ship sailing through a sea of darkness. Although she lived in the house all my years at Dunlossit, I had rarely spoken to her as she seemed so distant and self-contained as if she did not need human company. She never married, perhaps because no man on the island could live up to her air of refinement. She would, from time to time, go home to stay with her mother who lived in a house outside Bruichladdich which looked across to Loch Indaal with Bowmore casting its intricate pattern of night lights on the other side of the sea.

Despite, or because of, the novelty of spending a night in the Big House, I got little sleep. When I did doze off, I was soon awakened by troubled dreams and I sat up on the unfamiliar bed with a start. The room in which my brother and I slept seemed so much darker than the box room I had left behind. Perhaps it was the thick, smothering curtains which deepened the darkness. If I listened closely, I could hear the sea making restless noises which sounded threatening, knowing that I would be sailing on it in the morning and the memory of the storm remained vivid in my mind and sometimes in my dreams. Having been so close to death makes one's hold on life seem more fragile and precarious. My need to pee made me get up but I could not find the bedside light, if there was one. I stumbled in the darkness, with outstretched arms, as if I had gone blind – awakening and finding that I had gone blind had long been a recurring nightmare for me. In the darkness, I groped my way to where I thought the door was but all I could feel was a wall where the door should be. It was as if I found myself in a room with no way out. All I could do was to stumble my way back into bed and wait for the coming of dawn to thin out the thick night. As I lay awake, I heard noises: the floorboards creaked as if under the pressure of heavy footsteps;

the hinges of the door I could not see and could not find, complained as if someone was trying to get in. Having a vivid imagination, made more vivid in my heightened emotional state, made me fearful of ghosts which I have always half-believed in. I found myself wondering how Marion could stay alone in this house of many rooms night after night, particularly in the storms of winter when every window, every door and every floorboard must make its own distinctive but unidentifiable noise.

Somehow that long night passed and the door was opened not by an apparition but by my father telling George – who somehow managed to sleep through the traumas of the night – and me that it was time to get up. I got out of bed feeling more exhausted than I had when I had climbed into it. I went into the unusually spacious, but still chilly, bathroom, relieved at being able to pee at last. I splashed cold water over my face and hurriedly dressed before I made my way down two flights of the wide staircase and into the kitchen where the rest of the family had already begun breakfast. I swallowed a few mouthfuls of cornflakes, feeling the weight of the spoon in my hand.

Before we made our way down to the pier, I walked up the drive to take a last look at our house which now stood abandoned. The windows looked strangely blank having lost their curtains and it was as if those windows were eyes which looked accusingly at me. The rain of the night had darkened the walls. I looked up at the small window of the box room through which I had so often looked through to survey the scene: my world, below. I half-expected to see my face at the window staring back at me as if to wave me goodbye. After all, I was saying goodbye not only to my house but to my childhood. I walked back down the drive on which the dead leaves were falling, slowly somersaulting through the grey, cold air which was curiously still in the gaps between the gasps of wind.

I do not remember if we got a lift with our heavy suitcases down to Port or if we walked. Parts of the morning are so vivid and yet other parts are so blurred as if I was moving in and out of consciousness or in and out of a trance. As we stood on the pier next to the shelter in which I had so often played in during the many afternoons of rain, I watched the *Lochiel* sidle into the pier. The lassoes were placed around the bollards by Duncan in his worn tweed cap. I heard the dripping ropes take the strain as the ferry shifted and strangled the bollards. Eventually, the wooden gangway was lowered and tied and then I saw the fortunate, disembarking passengers set foot on the island which I was about to leave, not knowing when, if ever, I was to return. When all the passengers had disembarked, some boarding the bus to Port Ellen and others boarding the one to Portnahaven where the seals would be lounging on the rocks in the horseshoe bay and making their haunting cries at the onset of dusk, we made our way up the gangway in single file, lugging our suitcases. Whereas the rest of the family headed for the lounge, my mother removing the newspaper from her bag in order to place on the seat to keep sea sickness at bay, I stood out on the deck and watched the only world I knew move away from me as the ferry reversed out from the pier before it began to move up the Sound. Through the grey, November air, I looked back at Freeport with plumes of smoke rising from the chimneys of the cottages to merge with the low clouds. I saw the pier move further away with that old uncertainty as to whether it was the ferry which was moving or the pier. I looked back at the whitewashed hotel with its yellow window frames and doors, knowing that I would never again sit on the wall outside the public bar on those evenings when the moored rowing boats in the bay rose and fell in a gentle swell.

I stood leaning on the rusted railings of the *Lochiel* and gazed at the lifeboat as it tugged at its anchor in the ship's wake. I looked up at the Big House with its shuttered windows. Then there was the Wee Pier where I so often stood with my weighted, orange line wavering in the sea in search of saithe. Then the ferry moved below the only house I had ever known, its windows like blinded eyes. I imagined the empty house echoing with those voices which would never return. Perhaps it would remain empty all through the winter if a replacement gardener could not be found until the spring, with the wind and rain beating against the panes of glass which would not cast their oblong of light on the grass or the flickering flames of the paraffin lamp when the power was cut. There would be no one to light a fire in the grate each morning and the cold and dampness would deepen in layers.

In many respects, I preferred to have our house stand empty as I did not like the thought of others living in it with their alien voices disturbing the familiar ghosts.

Then came the small lighthouse with its jetty on which I stood alone that evening when I pulled that exotic orange fish from the sea but could not land it. That lost fish seemed now like a symbol for all the precious moments I could not hold on to and which would never come again. I went on standing on the deck despite the chilly wind which numbed my face and which only partly dried my tears as the turbine house came into view, its windows peering out from between the clump of trees whose roots reached so close to the shore. I saw the rounded rocks where my mother, George and I would sit on those rare picnic outings in summer when my mother had the time and the energy to escape from the demanding domestic drudgery of her days and find a few moments of release from her island prison. She would sit on the rock and listen to the flow of the water as it merged with the sea and sometimes watch a heron stand motionless and with endless patience as it waited for the right moment to strike with the sword of its beak. As the ferry left the turbine house behind and moved further up the coast, I sensed that my island territory was being left further and further behind. It was fading like the distant wake behind the ferry. Soon, MacArthur's Head lighthouse surrounded by its whitewashed walls appeared and the outline of Islay was being gradually erased like the movement of a rubber over pencilled lines or like the chalk dusted off the blackboard in Keills Primary school as I sat on the back row gazing out of the window at the long grass waving, and the crows perched on the stone wall of the playground staring back at me. Those pencilled lines on paper and those chalk marks on the blackboard can never be wholly erased, the outlines of what has been written remain and you feel the need to decipher them to discover who you are. The past comes to glow more brightly like the flashes of a distant lighthouse which form circles of light across sea and land as darkness deepens and which seem to beckon more urgently as the years pass.